Peter Szondi is widely regarded as  war literary critics. This first Eng interesting series of lectures, trar foreword by Joel Weinsheimer, English-speaking readers.

The question of what is involved in understanding a text and legal scholars long before it became a concern of literary critics. Szondi here traces the development of hermeneutics through examination of the work of eighteenth-century German scholars. Ordinarily treated only as prefigurations of Schleiermacher, the work of Enlightenment theorists Johann Martin Chladenius, Georg Friedrich Meier, and Friedrich Ast yields valuable insight into the "material theory" of interpretation — an epistemology of understanding on which a practical interpretive methodology might be built.

❖❖

Introduction to literary hermeneutics

Literature, Culture, Theory

❖❖❖❖❖❖❖❖❖❖❖❖❖❖❖❖❖❖❖❖❖❖❖❖❖❖❖❖❖❖❖❖❖❖❖❖❖❖❖

General editors

RICHARD MACKSEY, *The Johns Hopkins University*
and MICHAEL SPRINKER, *State University of New York at Stony Brook*

The Cambridge *Literature, Culture, Theory* series is dedicated to theoretical studies in the human sciences that have literature and culture as their object of enquiry. Acknowledging the contemporary expansion of cultural studies and the redefinitions of literature that this has entailed, the series includes not only original works of literary theory but also monographs and essay collections on topics and seminal figures from the long history of theoretical speculation on the arts and human communication generally. The concept of theory embraced in the series is broad, including not only the classical disciplines of poetics and rhetoric, but also those of aesthetics, linguistics, psychoanalysis, semiotics, and other cognate sciences that have inflected the systematic study of literature during the past half century.

Titles published

Return to Freud: Jacques Lacan's dislocation of psychoanalysis
SAMUEL WEBER
(*translated from the German by Michael Levine*)

Wordsworth, dialogics, and the practice of criticism
DON H. BIALOSTOSKY

The subject of modernity
ANTHONY J. CASCARDI

Onomatopoetics: theory of language and literature
JOSEPH GRAHAM

Parody: ancient, modern, and post-modern
MARGARET A. ROSE

The poetics of personification
JAMES PAXSON

Possible worlds in literary theory
RUTH RONEN

Critical conditions:
Postmodernity and the question of foundations
HORACE L. FAIRLAMB

Introduction to literary hermeneutics
PETER SZONDI
(*translated from the German by Martha Woodmansee*)

Introduction to literary hermeneutics

❖❖❖

PETER SZONDI

translated from the German by

MARTHA WOODMANSEE

Case Western Reserve University

Published by the Press Syndicate of the University of Cambridge
The Pitt Building, Trumpington Street, Cambridge, CB2 1RP
40 West 20th Street, New York, NY 10011-4211, USA
10 Stamford Road, Oakleigh, Melbourne 3166, Australia

First published 1995

Printed in Great Britain at the University Press, Cambridge

A catalogue record for this book is available from the British Library

Library of Congress cataloguing in publication data

Szondi, Peter
[Einführung in die literarische Hermeneutik. English]
Introduction to literary hermeneutics / Peter Szondi: translated from the German by
Martha Woodmansee.
p.   cm. – (Literature, culture, theory)
Includes bibliographical references and index.
ISBN 0 521 30111 4 (hardback)   ISBN 0 521 45931 1 (paperback)
1. Hermeneutics.   I. Title.   II. Series.
PN81.S9513   1994   93-28757
801'.95–dc20   CIP

ISBN 0 521 30111 4 hardback
ISBN 0 521 45931 1 paperback

Contents

Chapter 10.   **Schleiermacher, II**   121

Foreword

by
JOEL WEINSHEIMER

What explains the persistence of hermeneutics? The broad-based resurgence of interpretation theory typified by Martha Woodmansee's translation of Peter Szondi's *Introduction to Literary Hermeneutics* is occurring precisely at the time when it might seem that hermeneutics, with theory generally, should be fading slowly over the horizon. During the seventies and eighties, talk about the "hermeneutic mafia" at Yale apparently identified hermeneutics with deconstruction. Yet hermeneutics seems to have survived the passing not only of structuralism but poststructuralism too. Besides retaining its long-standing foothold in theology, jurisprudence, and history, hermeneutics has in recent times seen the efflorescence of new "interpretivist" movements in political science, anthropology, rhetoric, and even economics. These movements have marked the expansion and indeed globalization of hermeneutics to the point that it is now perceived to comprehend all the human sciences and (after Kuhn) the natural sciences as well.

The fact that hermeneutics has survived and prospered within the realm of literary studies – indeed gaining new energy from the "against theory" movement – becomes more understandable when we recall that (however identified in the popular mind with hermeneutics) structuralism and deconstruction, as well as Foucauldian discourse analysis, explicitly defined themselves as antihermeneutical. Both of the former were based in great part on structural linguistics, and as Jonathan Culler pointed out, "linguistics is not hermeneutic. It does not discover what a sequence means or produce a new interpretation of it but tries to determine the nature of the system underlying the event."[1] Since "the fabrication of meaning is more important ... than the meanings themselves," Roland Barthes ex-

---

[1] *Structuralist Poetics* (Ithaca: Cornell University Press, 1975), p. 31.

plained that the structuralist activity was designed "less to assign completed meanings to the objects it discovers than to know how meaning is possible."[2] And writing of Nietzschean deconstruction, Derrida proclaims, "The hermeneutic project which postulates a true sense of the text is disqualified under this regime .... The veil [is] no more raised than it is lowered." "Thus," he concludes, "the Schleiermachers and the veilmakers are routed."[3] So too in their *Michel Foucault* Dreyfus and Rabinow tell us that "Foucault was never tempted by the search for deep meaning" any more than by the structuralist attempt to describe its mere possibility. Shortly before his death, Foucault was "planning to write an 'archaeology of hermeneutics.' ... Fragments of this project are evident in some of his writings on Nietzsche."[4] Thus the authors situate Foucauldian analysis "beyond structuralism and hermeneutics."

For literature, the rise of antihermeneutic theory in the seventies registered the fact that criticism, as then practiced, had become mechanical, unreflective, and dull. "One thing we do not need is more interpretation of literary works," Culler wrote in 1981,[5] and he was certainly right insofar as interpreting meant writing more New Critical "readings." Yet the alternative impulse toward poetics and away from interpretation hardly meant that the Schleiermachers were routed. The many other kinds and venues of interpretation — on stage, for instance, or in translation — were as little affected by the fall of formalist theory as by the rise of postmodernism. And literary hermeneutics never really ceased, though it did metamorphose by changing its object. No longer literature, the preferred object of interpretation during the last two decades became literary theory itself, so that "readings" of Derrida proliferated as wildly as had those of Donne twenty years before. This is not to suggest that the interpretation of literature ceased either. Understanding Proust and Hölderlin became, if anything, even more urgent. Although Paul de Man warned that "the possibility of reading can never be taken for granted,"[6] it could not go

[2] "The Structuralist Activity," in *Critical Theory since Plato*, ed. Hazard Adams (New York: Harcourt Brace Jovanovich, 1971), p. 1198.
[3] *Spurs: Nietzsche's Styles*, tr. Barbara Harlow (Chicago: University of Chicago Press, 1978), pp. 107 and 129.
[4] Hubert L. Dreyfus and Paul Rabinow, *Michel Foucault: Beyond Structuralism and Hermeneutics*, 2nd edn. (Chicago: University of Chicago Press, 1983), p. xii.
[5] *The Pursuit of Signs: Semiotics, Literature, Deconstruction* (Ithaca: Cornell University Press, 1981), p. 6.
[6] *Blindness and Insight: Essays in the Rhetoric of Contemporary Criticism* (New York: Oxford University Press, 1971), p. 107.

unnoticed for long that he himself produced magnificent readings of literature which, though hardly New Critical, could just as aptly be described as hyperformalist as deconstructive. Indeed, it seems pointless to deny that *Of Grammatology* was itself an interpretation of Rousseau, albeit of a special kind.

More recently, as deconstruction has itself metamorphosed into cultural criticism, the object of literary interpretation has altered in another respect. Not only has concern with the nonappropriative understanding of Otherness reinvigorated hermeneutic inquiry into the nature of understanding. Interest has shifted from what a work portrays to what it betrays — typically, the concealed power differentials operative between genders, races, and classes. Yet reading against the grain remains a kind of reading. What Ricoeur calls "the hermeneutics of suspicion"[7] remains a kind of hermeneutics, indeed one with a venerable tradition that can be traced back through ideology critique, psychoanalysis, and Marxism at least as far as Spinoza.[8] The cultural criticism that works to penetrate dark secrets and reveal the hidden truth — that understands its task as exposing the dogshit upon which the palace of culture is erected (in Horkheimer's delicate phrase) — such criticism reinstates precisely the hermeneutic regime of unveiling that Derrida declared defunct.

Hermeneutics has persisted in part because it is so protean and polymorphous that if repressed in one form it returns in another. The defect of this virtue is that hermeneutics is, logically speaking, indeterminate and amorphous. "Nothing is definable that has a history," Nietzsche somewhere remarks. Hermeneutics has meant so many things over the last two decades, not to mention the last two centuries, or the last two millennia, that any definition must be either vague, partial, or misleading. In good part this explains why Szondi's *Introduction to Literary Hermeneutics* necessarily takes a historical rather than systematic form.

In designing his introduction historically, Szondi follows Wilhelm Dilthey, whose seminal essay "The Development of Hermeneutics" charted the history of interpretation theory in a way that influenced every subsequent historian. "I shall document this orderly progress," Dilthey writes, "by showing how philological virtuosity arose from the need for deep and valid understanding. This gave rise to rules

---

[7] See *Freud and Philosophy*, tr. Denis Savage (New Haven: Yale University Press, 1970).

[8] On Spinoza's hermeneutics, see Tzvetan Todorov, *Symbolism and Interpretation*, tr. Catherine Porter (Ithaca: Cornell University Press, 1982).

which were purposefully organized and systematized according to the state of scholarship in a given period, and finally an assured starting-point for making these rules was found in the analysis of under-standing."[9] Several aspects of Dilthey's synopsis are pertinent to clarifying the thrust of Szondi's project. First, Dilthey plots the history of hermeneutics teleologically, as an "orderly progress" whose end is to arrive at "an assured starting-point" for hermeneutics proper. Second, he depicts the progress of interpretive certainty as a movement from practice to theory. More specifically, on Dilthey's account interpretation begins with intuitive good sense; then intuition is systematized in rules abstracted from its practice; and finally, hermeneutics climaxes at a still further remove from the activity of interpreting, when the rules themselves dissolve into the universal philosophy of understanding initiated by Schleiermacher.

Szondi disputes this schema in every respect but its historicality, and even that is not sufficiently historical by far. To plot the history of hermeneutics as a progress toward Schleiermacher is to obviate the study of both prior and subsequent history. It subordinates Schleier-macher's Enlightenment predecessors to the role of dim prefigurations, and his modern successors to the role of belated epigones. For Szondi much substantial, new work still remains to be done. We will consider it in a moment. But the point here is that since in Szondi's view substantial innovation cannot be brought about merely by fleshing out Schleiermacher's hermeneutics, it becomes necessary to point out the inadequacies of Schleiermacher as a prelude to disclosing and avoiding the deficiencies of the tradition stemming from him, including Dilthey, Heidegger, and Gadamer.

Szondi's *Introduction to Literary Hermeneutics*, then, is an expressly critical exposition. Yet it does not proceed unhistorically by basing its critique of hermeneutic history on a new system created *ex nihilo*. Rather, Szondi tries to move beyond the hermeneutic tradition of Schleiermacher by reexamining its prehistory and determining what of value the march of progress denigrated, ignored, or overlooked. Thus the *Introduction*'s central chapters offer an intensive examination of authors and works retrieved from the oblivion into which Dilthey's teleology had cast them: specifically, Chladenius' *Einleitung zur richtigen Auslegung vernünftiger Reden und Schriften* (1742), Meier's *Versuch einer allgemeinen Auslegungskunst* (1757), and Ast's *Grundlinien*

---

[9] *Dilthey: Selected Writings*, ed. H. P. Richman (Cambridge: Cambridge University Press, 1976), pp. 249–50.

der Grammatik, Hermeneutik und Kritik (1808). In each case – in Meier's notion of hermeneutic equity, for example, or Ast's nonaggregative notion of parts as an unfolding (or explication) of the whole – Szondi finds hermeneutic insights of genuine value. His interest is not merely historical, for in writing a critical history he means always to learn from these figures, even from their mistakes.

For Szondi, then, Schleiermacher's philosophy of understanding represents neither the beginning of hermeneutics proper nor the climax of its history. It is not the beginning because examination of Enlightenment and early Romantic hermeneutics shows that Dilthey's thesis is untenable: universal hermeneutics conceived as analysis of understanding did not begin with Schleiermacher but still earlier. Even if it did, however, philosophical hermeneutics hardly marks the climax and fruition of hermeneutic thought, for the retreat from hermeneutic practice and the approach toward hermeneutic philosophy in Szondi's view represents no progress. Quite the contrary, philosophical hermeneutics in the tradition of Schleiermacher precludes development of just the kind of literary hermeneutics that Szondi considers most necessary.

As he envisions it, the new hermeneutics should be not only critical and historical, as we have seen, but also practical and genre-specific. It should be practical, first, in the sense of being applicable, and guiding interpretive practice. According to Dilthey, Schleiermacher's analysis of understanding was meant to offer an "assured starting-point" for devising rules which, scrupulously followed, made valid interpretation possible. But even if Schleiermacher's own hermeneutics retained the practicality of an interpretive *organon*, the philosophical hermeneutics deriving from it, Szondi charges, typically disdained the formulation of rules and hence the road to praxis. Like Kant's critique of reason, the critique of interpretation after Schleiermacher disclosed the conditions and limits of understanding but resulted in no *ars interpretandi*. Philosophical hermeneutics failed in offering what Szondi wants first of all from hermeneutics: a "material theory" of interpretation that would not skip in Heidegger's manner from unsystematized interpretive knowhow to the grandeur of hermeneutic ontology. Like Ricœur, Szondi refused to minimize the need for an epistemology of understanding on which a practical interpretive methodology could be built.[10]

[10] Cf. Paul Ricœur, "Existence and Hermeneutics" (tr. Kathleen McLaughlin), in *Contemporary Hermeneutics: Hermeneutics as Method, Philosophy, and Critique*, ed. Josef Bleicher (London: Routledge, 1980), pp. 236–56.

Szondi's new hermeneutics, moreover, is to be "genre-specific." As indicated prominently in Szondi's title, his is an introduction to *literary* hermeneutics. "The fact that a specifically literary hermeneutics scarcely exists today," Szondi rightly argues, "stems rather from the nature of the hermeneutics that actually does exist" (p. 1). Hermeneutics in the modern tradition was designed precisely to be nonspecific. Whereas Chladenius insists on the differences between scriptural and philological interpretation, for example, the fairness that Meier calls *aequitas hermeneutica* is appropriate and necessary regardless what kind of text is being interpreted, whether literary or not. So also Meier, following Schelling, posits a universally shared *Geist* as the condition of understanding anything whatever, and Schleiermacher formulated his own ambition as moving beyond regional to a general hermeneutics on which *hermeneutica sacra* and *profana* alike were to be based. In this night all cows are black, Szondi suggests. By virtue of its universality, philosophical hermeneutics conceived as analysis of understanding homogenizes its objects and irons over their differences.

By contrast to this universality, Szondi calls for the development of a genre-specific, and particularly literature-specific, hermeneutics. In this respect he can be profitably compared with Emilio Betti. The generality of Betti's *General Theory of Interpretation* consists not in being universal but rather comprehensively multi-regional.[11] Betti postulates three fundamental types of interpretation: cognitive, performative, and normative, corresponding respectively to, for example, a historical event, a musical score, and a legal statute. Yet Betti's typology classifies kinds – not objects – of interpretation, as Szondi would prefer. If the business of a judge is to understand a statute in the "normative" way by applying it to a particular case, the same statute might be interpreted "cognitively" by a historian who merely wanted to know its meaning or origin. Still more clearly, literature is not limited to any of the three types of interpretation Betti lists. A play can be explicated in a scholarly article, performed on stage, or applied by the spectators (as the phrase goes) to their daily lives. Thus Betti's trichotomy does not answer the call for a literature-specific hermeneutics.

---

[11] Betti's hermeneutics is conveniently accessible in his summary, "Hermeneutics as the General Methodology of the *Geisteswissenschaften*," tr. Josef Bleicher, in *Contemporary Hermeneutics: Hermeneutics as Method, Philosophy, and Critique* (London: Routledge, 1980), pp. 51–94.

Closer to fulfilling Szondi's desiderata is E. D. Hirsch's principle: "valid interpretation is always governed by a valid inference about genre." By 'genre' Hirsch means just what Szondi does: not only that the correct understanding of *Gulliver's Travels*, say, depends on knowing whether it is a novel or a satire, but also knowing that Gibbon's *Decline and Fall* is history whereas Evelyn Waugh's is literature. Hirsch allies himself with Wellek and Warren in insisting that "the study of literature ought to be literary, just as the study and interpretation of philosophical texts ought to be philosophical. Behind this programmatic idea is a notion of validity: the literary study of literature is not simply an appropriate mode of interpretation; it is the only really valid mode."[12] For Hirsch, we recall, the interpreter's inference about the work's literariness or its subgenre ultimately amounts to an inference about its intrinsic genre: the author's intention. But that is not the direction Szondi wants to go. The principle that interpretation must be guided by intention and genre can hardly claim to be genre-specific, and in any case Hirsch expressly denies that its corollary (literary study should be literary) yields anything at all by way of practical rules or methodology.

It is not primarily Betti and Hirsch, however, but rather Hans-Georg Gadamer who most clearly represents for Szondi the inadequacy of modern philosophical hermeneutics; and the *Introduction to Literary Hermeneutics* can fruitfully be read as an underground polemic with *Truth and Method* that frequently erupts to the surface. For Szondi, we have seen, hermeneutics has become so preoccupied with analysis of understanding that it has come to consider itself superior to its one-time task of being a material theory concerned with the rules and criteria of interpretation (p. 3). No one fits this charge better than Gadamer: "The purpose of my investigation," he writes, "is not to offer a general theory of interpretation and a differential account of its methods." "I did not wish to elaborate a system of rules to describe, let alone direct, the methodical procedure of the human sciences. Nor was it my aim to investigate the theoretical foundation of work in these fields in order to put my findings to practical ends."[13]

Likewise *Truth and Method* implicitly downgrades what had been the paradigmatic status of philological (and hence literary) hermeneutics, finding "exemplary significance" in legal hermeneutics

---

[12] *Validity in Interpretation* (New Haven: Yale University Press, 1967), pp. 112–13.
[13] *Truth and Method*, 2nd rev. edn., tr. Joel Weinsheimer and Donald G. Marshall (New York: Crossroad, 1989), pp. xxxi and xxviii.

instead. When Gadamer belatedly comes to discuss literature, moreover, we find that even then it is not *Dichtung* but *Literatur* that concerns him, not the aesthetic quality of literariness but rather readability as a mode of intelligibility by no means confined to literature alone. Szondi's pronouncement that the new "literary hermeneutics will make the text's aesthetic character a premise of interpretation" (p. 4) directly contradicts Gadamer's pronouncement that "aesthetics must dissolve into hermeneutics."[14] It can hardly be surprising therefore that Szondi considers Gadamer's hermeneutics as an impediment to the construction of his own.

What Szondi means by the "aesthetic character" of literature becomes clear in his critique of Chladenius' mimetic assumption: "The possibility that a literary work might not have preexisting subjects but that these subjects might be brought into being by the work, or might be identical with it, was necessarily inconceivable to a hermeneutics that remained within the framework of the *imitatio naturae* theory" (p. 45). "The overthrow of [the mimetic theory] in the late eighteenth century brought, as it were, a new point of view to power, which continues to condition our understanding of literature today. It is thus impossible to bracket out the more recent view according to which literature creates its own object" (p. 58). That is to say, after Kant, Chladenius' mimetic hermeneutics could not be adapted, without substantial revision, to the needs of an aesthetically oriented theory of interpretation, for Kant overthrew mimeticism when he showed that taste or aesthetic judgment is subjective not objective (there is no prior object to which the beautiful is compared) and, correlatively, that the imagination of genius is creative (it creates its own object). Thus a genre-specific literary hermeneutics – in Szondi's view, one premised on the aesthetic character of literature – could not conceive of itself mimetically. The object of literary understanding is nothing but the work – not some meaning, prior object, or independent subject matter that might be common to other works as well.

Thus to Szondi it seems that Gadamer is formulating (in a passage Szondi cites) not just a nonaesthetic but indeed an antiaesthetic hermeneutics: "Understanding means, primarily, to understand the content of what is said, and only secondarily to isolate and understand another's meaning as such. Hence the most basic of all hermeneutic preconditions remains one's own fore-understanding, which comes

[14] Ibid., p. 164.

from being concerned with the same subject ... Thus the meaning of 'belonging' – i.e., the element of tradition in our historical–hermeneutical activity – is fulfilled in the commonality of fundamental, enabling prejudices."[15]

Szondi is undoubtedly correct to imply that Gadamer's hermeneutics is mimetic. With respect to drama, in fact, Gadamer speaks of a "double mimesis." The actors mime on stage what the playwright mimes in print. If the performance constitutes a genuine interpretation of the play, then the meaning of the play coincides with the meaning of its faithful presentation as well. It is common to them both – otherwise the performance would amount to a new play and not an interpretation. Yet it is also the case that interpretive novelty is not a defect but a value. Ideally each interpretation brings something new to the play that lets us see it as it is, as if for the first time. Just like really vital traditions, and as an instance of them, the very best interpretations are both mimetic and creative, always conservative, always innovative. Now, for Gadamer to say that the play too constitutes an interpretation – of the world, or life, if you prefer – is to imply that it too mimes something prior to it, just as the play exists prior to the performance of it. Yet in the same way, too, a play that lets us understand for the first time something we have known all along joins poesis and mimesis. It must be called not just imitative but creative as well – and creative in a sense that cannot be dichotomized from imitation.

By contrast to Gadamer's, Szondi's aesthetic hermeneutics is based on just that dichotomy. Gadamer's notion of "double mimesis" means that the relation of the interpretation to the work is the same as that of the work to the world: i.e., at the same time mimetic and creative – or, in a word, interpretive. Since art in Gadamer's view is just as interpretive as the interpretation of it, his hermeneutics necessarily forgoes the possibility of any specifically aesthetic hermeneutics. But then its whole point is to affirm that all creation as well as all understanding is mimetic, interpretive, traditionary: always dependent on precedent while always transforming it as well.

For Szondi, on the other hand, a literature-specific hermeneutics would conceptualize a kind of interpretation which respects the fact that literary art is creative – i.e., it has no prior object or content. Literary interpretation, like all interpretation, of course, is necessarily

[15] Ibid., pp. 294–95.

object-oriented: it is an interpretation of something. Interpretation is always mimetic, then, but Szondi must deny that it is creative as well, since then it would approximate art, and the possibility of a special aesthetic hermeneutics would be lost. In Szondi's view, therefore, literature-specific interpretation cannot itself be literary, for literature is not itself interpretive. A categorical divide forever separates the two. The literary interpretation of literature, however tautological that sounds, must mean the mimesis of what is no mimesis, the interpretation of what is not itself an interpretation. Given this antithesis, two consequences follow: Gadamerian talk of understanding as fusion must be mistaken, and given that literature is nonmimetic, understanding literature cannot mean understanding what it is about, its content.

Szondi's neo-Kantian resistance to mimeticism bears directly on his second desideratum for hermeneutics — namely that it offer methodologically grounded rules. The connection becomes evident when we recall that Kant's *Critique of Judgment* presents a second conception of aesthetic creativity, one defined by the absence not of a prior object but of rules. "There can be no objective rule of taste, no rule of taste that determines by concepts what is beautiful ... If we search for a principle of taste that states the universal criterion of the beautiful by means of determinate concepts, then we engage in a fruitless endeavor, because we search for something that is impossible and intrinsically contradictory."[16] Both the reception of art (taste) and the production of art (genius) are creative in that they do not follow rules. They create them.

In respect to this definition of creativity, too, Szondi aligns himself with Kant against Gadamer. When Gadamer advocates dissolving aesthetics into hermeneutics, this does not at all mean the elimination of the aesthetic, but only the aesthetic proper, since with that dissolution *all* hermeneutics becomes aesthetical. Gadamer declines to formulate a system of hermeneutic rules, not because he disdains the task, but because collapsing aesthetic judgment into pure reason, as it were, makes interpretation a mode of understanding governed by no rules, just like taste itself. In Gadamer's view what determines the validity of interpretation is hermeneutic taste, not a criterion. Szondi, just the opposite, preserves the distinction between the first and third critiques. By the same argument as outlined above, therefore, this

[16] *Critique of Judgment*, tr. Werner S. Pluhar (Indianapolis: Hackett, 1987), p. 79.

distinction implies that a specifically aesthetic hermeneutics would not be aesthetic itself: it would consist in the rule-governed interpretation of what is itself governed by no rules. Understanding literature cannot mean, as Gadamer said, making sense of the subject matter, for art has no content; instead, it means following the rules. Rather than fusion, understanding means correctness.

Where Szondi differs most from Kant is in respect to genre. He insists on the "real diversity of the texts" (p. 16), and on the ways "various types of writing are distinguished from one another – historical from literary, but also within literature the individual genres" (p. 46). Szondi considers both literariness in general and individual genre qualities as "real" – i.e., intrinsic to literary works – rather than as hypostatized "approaches" or frameworks of expectation. We need not dwell on the fact that genre, the principle meant to guide interpretation, cannot be discovered except through interpretation, since Szondi repeatedly shows himself aware of this problem (e.g., pp. 81, 82, 83). More interesting in situating Szondi within a Kantian context is the question whether the "real diversity of texts" is limited to diversity of genres.

"In their logical quantity all judgments of taste are *singular* judgments," Kant writes.[17] Taste judges particular instances of the beautiful, not kinds. That is why judging beauty has no rules, and aesthetic judgment can be learned only by appeal to examples, not precepts or concepts. Every instance of beauty is singular; but every concept, law, or rule – and certainly every genre – covers a multitude of instances. Decisive in overthrowing neoclassical rule-based aesthetics was Kant's insight that specifically aesthetic judgment concerns itself with unique, unrepeatable phenomena, whereas all rules, not just those concerned with genre, are generic. With respect to literature, then, a Kantian would argue against Szondi that generic diversity, however important to recognize, must ultimately conceal the "real diversity of texts." It is pure reason, not aesthetic judgment, that conceives of understanding as subsumption under rules, laws, kinds, and genres. Generic interpretation achieves correctness by subsuming diversity into homogeneity.

Szondi clearly does recognize the need for specifically aesthetic understanding, however, as well as for understanding of specifically aesthetic objects. With Schleiermacher, he acknowledges that genre is

[17] Ibid., p. 59.

a rule "'whose successful application depends on the interpreter's sensitivity'" (p. 124). If a rule, genre is no better or worse than a crude rule of thumb, and applying it without sensitivity can produce only crude interpretations. The required sensitivity or aesthetic sensibility is an attentiveness to just that uniqueness of the text wherein it exceeds the rule and consequently cannot be understood by appeal to it. As Szondi remarks elsewhere, "[literary] texts present themselves as individuals, not as specimens."[18] Yet he cannot go too far in this direction because the need for sensitivity to unsubsumable individuality, even if we insist on calling it aesthetic, cannot be limited to literature, or art, or the beautiful alone.

Meier, for instance, draws his notion of fairness or *aequitas hermeneutica* from the legal sphere because jurisprudence since Aristotle had perceived the inadequacy of subsumption. Equitable interpretation is necessary in adapting general laws to individual cases. Just decisions are those made on the basis of laws, no doubt; but unjust interpretations can be made on that basis too: as the maxim has it, *summum jus, summa injuria* (greatest law, greatest injury). Hence the need for fairness, for attention to special circumstances, in coming to an equitable decision. The immediately relevant point is that justice, like beauty, cannot be decided on the basis of rules alone. To cite one of Meier's British contemporaries, the jurist William Blackstone: "equity thus depending upon the particular circumstances of each individual case, there can be no established rules and fixed precepts of equity laid down, without destroying its very essence."[19] In equitable interpretation of the law, which pays attention to the particular case at hand, justice is achieved by precisely that aesthetic judgment which obeys no law.

Could not the same argument be extended to historical understanding as well? On the one hand, a hermeneutics based on appeal to genre does not differ in logical form from one based on the spirit of the age; both can recognize diversity – among different periods, for example – though there remain further levels of variety and par-

---

[18] "On Textual Understanding," in *On Textual Understanding and Other Essays*, tr. Harvey Mendelsohn (Minneapolis: University of Minnesota Press, 1986), p. 13.

[19] *Commentaries on the Laws of England*, 4 vols. in 2, ed. William Carey Jones (San Francisco: Bancroft-Whitney, 1915), vol. 1, p. 61. For a discussion of Blackstone's theory of legal interpretation, see my *Eighteenth-Century Hermeneutics: Philosophy of Interpretation in England from Locke to Burke* (New Haven: Yale University Press, 1983), ch. 6.

ticularity they cannot reach. Szondi takes cognizance of that limitation most directly in his critique of Ast's notion of spirit: "as that which makes understanding possible (since all things are originally one in spirit and everything spiritual is originally one and the same), also guarantees a solution to all hermeneutic problems posed by factual differences" (p. 100). If "the spirit of the age" is useful for historical interpretation, it would seem that the spirit of humanity, or world spirit, or universal spirit, would be most useful of all, since it would make possible the understanding not just of one age but all.

Yet, as Szondi shows, the fact is just the opposite. Ast's universal spirit does not explain the possibility of historical understanding but obviates it, for understanding history ultimately means understanding the historical particular in its particularity. It is admittedly helpful to know that such and such events belong to the genre "Revolution," that they conform to the law of supply and demand, or that they are an expression of the "Romantic spirit." But historiography does not stop there, with general types and categories. It discriminates between this revolution and that, and not only between various expressions of Romanticism but various Romanticisms. If the object of aesthetic judgment is the unique work, and the object of jurisprudential equity is the particular circumstance, history too essentially requires sensitivity to detail, nuance, and difference. Understanding always means understanding the particularity of something.

Szondi's implicit realization of this fact, I think, best explains his insistence on diversity, and his resistance to universalist hermeneutics in the tradition of Schleiermacher. Whether and how he would have worked out the implications of a hermeneutics of particularity, we will unfortunately never know, since he did not live to complete the course of lectures on which his *Introduction* is based. Though Szondi did not move beyond the stage of critical history to develop systematically the literary hermeneutics he envisioned, we can nevertheless be grateful for his having critically reanimated a few figures from the forgotten history of interpretation theory, thereby reminding us that literary hermeneutics has not only a vital past but an open future as well.

Joel Weinsheimer, University of Minnesota, Minneapolis

Translator's preface

Still growing interest in hermeneutics notwithstanding, the texts that constitute its history, especially its "prehistory" prior to Schleiermacher, remain little known, because relatively inaccesible, to English readers. Peter Szondi's introduction to hermeneutics, with its attention to what eighteenth-century German hermeneutic scholars may still have to teach us, will help to remedy this situation.

Szondi was born in Budapest on May 27, 1929, to the well-known psychologist Leopold Szondi. The family fled to Switzerland in the 1930s. The young Szondi's studies, chiefly at the University of Zurich where he came under the influence of Emil Staiger, led in 1961 to a professorship at the Free University of Berlin. Soon thereafter he was appointed director of the university's Institute for General and Comparative Literature, a post he retained until his death, by his own hand, on October 18, 1971. In this capacity he welcomed scholars from Starobinski, Goldmann, and Bourdieu to Derrida, de Man, and Hartman, placing the Institute in the vanguard of poststructuralist ferment. His complex intellectual affiliations, which also included Lukács, Benjamin, and Adorno, are best pursued by consulting the special issue of *boundary 2* (Volume XI, Number 3 [Spring 1983]) that grew out of a colloquium organized to honor Szondi's work in 1978.

Szondi's books include his dissertation, *Theorie des modernen Dramas* (1956), available in an English translation by Michael Hays (*Theory of the Modern Drama* [Minneapolis: University of Minnesota Press, 1987]), *Versuch über das Tragische* (1961), *Hölderlin-Studien* (1967), *Celan-Studien* (1972), and several volumes of essays, a selection of which has been translated by Harvey Mendelsohn (*On Textual Understanding and Other Essays* [Minneapolis: University of Minnesota Press, 1986]). His complete works were reissued in two volumes by Suhrkamp Verlag (*Schriften I, II* [1978]), which also brought out a five-volume collection of his lecture notes ("Studienausgabe der Vorlesungen" [1974–75]).

Introduction to Literary Hermeneutics is taken from the fifth volume of lectures, edited by Jean Bollack and Helen Stierlin (1975). This volume also includes a set of lectures on "Problems of Interpretation," which address some of the same questions as the *Introduction* but in the practical context of a discussion of Hölderlin's *Feiertagshymne* and *Friedensfeier*. The *Introduction*, taught in the winter semester 1967–68, was originally to have continued into the modern period and to have covered Droysen, Dilthey, Benjamin, and Gadamer. However, radical student protest against conditions at the universities, including the venerable institution of the lecture course, caused the sympathetic Szondi to change plans and, in the interest of establishing an ongoing forum for the discussion of fundamental questions of literary-theoretical interest, to offer a colloquium on "Historical Understanding – Historicity of Knowledge" instead.

A translation of the first chapter of *Introduction*, by Timothy Bahti, appeared in *New Literary History* 10 (1978): 17–29. Portions of the last two chapters of the *Lectures* were revised for an essay, "L'hermé-neutique de Schleiermacher," which appeared in the French of S. Buguet in *Poétique* 2 (1970): 141–55. An English translation by Harvey Mendelsohn is included in the selection of Szondi's essays, *On Textual Understanding and Other Essays* (Minneapolis: University of Minnesota Press, 1986), pp. 95–113.

I wish to thank Ruth Ann Crowley and Fred Thompson for their very substantial help with the first draft of this translation and Patricia Harkin, Richard T. Gray, Sabine Wilke, and Joel Weinsheimer for their many valuable comments on the final draft. Werner J. Dannhauser's painstaking reading, in particular, prevented many an error from seeing the light of day.

Martha Woodmansee, Case Western Reserve University

I

Introduction

Literary hermeneutics is the theory of the exegesis, *interpretatio* or interpretation, of literary works. Although hermeneutics has been highly influential in shaping philosophy and, as self-reflection, humanistic inquiry in general in this century, it is not at all certain whether a specifically literary hermeneutics exists at present. Wilhelm Dilthey's essay "The Development of Hermeneutics" appeared in 1900; a significant part of his œuvre is devoted to developing a theory of understanding, especially historical understanding, to serve as a foundation for humanistic inquiry. In Heidegger's *Being and Time* (1927) an important place is given to the analysis of understanding as an "existential concern" as well as to the presentation of the "hermeneutic circle" and the rootedness of this circle in the "existential constitution of Dasein [*human existence*] – that is, in the understanding which interprets."[1] Gadamer's *Truth and Method* appeared three decades later, in 1960; its subtitle is "Essentials of a Philosophical Hermeneutics." Finally, in 1967, Emilio Betti's work *Teoria generale della interpretazione* (1955) appeared in German translation. Hermeneutics is therefore hardly a neglected discipline. Nor have the humanities or indeed literary studies resisted or dismissed the stimulus of Dilthey, Heidegger, and Gadamer. The fact that a specifically literary hermeneutics scarcely exists today stems rather from the nature of the hermeneutics that actually does exist.

Dilthey's essay of 1900, which reviews the rise of hermeneutics in programmatic fashion, posits that hermeneutics developed in an orderly way. The art of interpretation, he writes, soon developed into an exposition of the rules governing interpretation.

And the discipline of hermeneutics arose from the conflict of these rules, from the struggle of various schools over the interpretation of vitally important

---

[1] Martin Heidegger, *Being and Time*, tr. John Macquarrie and Edward Robinson (London, 1962), p. 195.

works and the consequent need to justify the rules of interpretation. It is the *theory of the art of interpretation of written artifacts [Schriftdenkmalen]*. Because this theory determines the possibility of universally valid interpretation on the basis of an analysis of understanding, it finally approaches a solution to the *wholly general problem* with which this discussion began. The analysis of understanding takes its place beside the analysis of inner experience to give proof of the *possibility* and the *limits* of universally valid knowledge in the humanities, insofar as this possibility and these limits are conditioned by the way in which psychological data are originally given.[2]

Dilthey's essay, which is often overvalued as a source of historical information,[3] aims to show

how philological virtuosity arose from the need for profound and universally valid understanding, how this virtuosity gave rise to the formulation of rules and to the ordering of rules with respect to a goal specified by the state of the discipline at a given time, until the secure basis for the formulation of rules was finally found in the analysis of understanding.[4]

There is no question but that the history of hermeneutics, from the Greeks and Alexandrians through the patristic tradition, the Middle Ages, Humanism, the Reformation and the Enlightenment to German Idealism, does exhibit such a development. Still, the "orderly course" that Dilthey posits[5] seems questionable. Of course, his presentation of its history does take into account "the state of the discipline *at a given time*." But the question remains whether this "orderly course" does not invalidate the idea of historical change which it is designed to encompass, by ignoring the historical element in the concept of understanding and the historicity of the rules. Hermeneutics was once exclusively a system of rules, while today it is exclusively a theory of understanding. This does not mean, however, that the old rules were not based on an unarticulated concept of understanding, nor that a theory of understanding today ought to forgo the formulation of rules — which is not the same thing as saying that the old rules are still valid.

[2] Wilhelm Dilthey, "The Development of Hermeneutics," in Dilthey, *Selected Writings*, ed., tr., and intro. H. P. Rickman (Cambridge, 1976), p. 249. I have emended Rickman's translation where it seemed appropriate.
[3] There exist much more valuable presentations such as G. Ebeling's article "Hermeneutik" in the encyclopedia *Die Religion in Geschichte und Gegenwart. Handwörterbuch für Theologie und Religionswissenschaft*, ed. Kurt Galling, 3rd edn. (Tübingen, 1957–65), vol. 3, cols. 242–62.
[4] Dilthey, "The Development of Hermeneutics," p. 250.   [5] Ibid., p. 249.

Historical change cannot be contained by the discovery, through progressive reformulation of the hermeneutic question, that analysis of understanding is "the secure basis for the establishment of rules." It is rather the case that the concept of understanding itself changes over time, as does the concept of the literary work; and this dual change should also result in a modification of the rules and criteria of interpretation, or at least necessitate their reexamination. But since hermeneutics, in the sense of the development traced by Dilthey — especially through his modification of the questions hermeneutics addresses — has increasingly become a discipline of basic principles, it has come to consider itself superior to its one-time task of being a material theory of interpretation.

For literary studies, insofar as the modern languages are concerned, this has quite different consequences than for classics, theology, or jurisprudence. These disciplines have a long hermeneutic tradition that they can revise at any time, but modern literary studies emerged after the turning point in hermeneutics, which Dilthey presents as the accomplishment of Schleiermacher: the way back behind the rules to an analysis of understanding. And while this philosophical turn was bound up in Schleiermacher's case with a continuation of material hermeneutics, outside the field of theology only the philosophical impulse continued to be active. Moreover, literary studies over the last hundred years — however contrary the tendencies that have conditioned them — have scarcely felt the need for a material hermeneutics. This is because of their premises. For Positivism facts about an author's life and works were givens whose intelligibility was not questioned. The intellectual history [*Geistesgeschichte*] shaped by Dilthey had recourse to his theory of the possibility of historical understanding; it paid less attention to the individual text than to the spirit of the age that spoke through the text; and since there was no question but that empathy provided access to this spirit, the interpretation of texts did not become problematic. Then began the age of interpretation, in which we seem still to be living and from which we should have expected, sooner than from Positivism or intellectual history, a revival of hermeneutics, of the *ars interpretandi*. But what the age of interpretation took from hermeneutics was little more than the name "the art of interpretation" and the concept of the hermeneutic circle.

The concept of the circle is of the greatest epistemological relevance for hermeneutics, with respect to both its philosophical foundation and its methodology. Yet when we examine the role played by the circle in contemporary critical practice, we see that it functions primarily to exempt interpretation from a critique of its own mode of cognition. The scandal of the circle, in which understanding must nonetheless recognize its very condition, has become a sedative. "What is decisive is not to get out of the circle, but to come into it in the right way"[6] is a thesis that undoubtedly has some validity. But Heidegger did not have to say it twice before all methodological questions and doubts were met with the blanket statement that we were moving within the hermeneutic circle. A material theory of interpretation, which might well be shaped throughout by the circularity of understanding, was not achieved by the practitioners of "the art of interpretation" either.[a] This calls itself an "art" in the archaic sense familiar to us from phrases like "the art of the fugue" — *ars interpretandi*, the *theory* of interpretation. However, this choice of terms has doubtless fostered the idea that interpretation is an art that one can at best demonstrate, but cannot teach, let alone submit to critical analysis along epistemological lines.

What Dilthey called the regular course of the history of hermeneutics, the development from a material to a philosophical hermeneutics, can nevertheless not be reversed. We cannot find the rules for a literary hermeneutics by looking to the past, to prephilosophical hermeneutics. If we speak of literary hermeneutics rather than of philological hermeneutics, it is primarily because the theory of interpretation we have in mind will have to differ from the traditional hermeneutics of classical philology. Instead of considering the aesthetic character of a text in an "appreciation" presented after the text has been interpreted, as does classical philology, literary hermeneutics will make the text's aesthetic character a premise of interpretation. That is, the traditional rules and criteria of philological interpretation must be revised in light of today's understanding of literature.

This suggests a further distinction between literary and philological hermeneutics. Literary hermeneutics is conscious of its own historicity

---

[6] Heidegger, *Being and Time*, p. 195.
[a] Allusion is to the Zurich school of interpretation founded by Emil Staiger. Staiger's influential *Die Kunst der Interpretation*, which appeared in 1955, draws on Heidegger to elaborate a highly subjective mode of interpretation. Cf. below, p. 131f.

and does not want to renounce it, whereas traditional, so-called historical philology believes that it can erase its own historical position and transport itself back into a period of the past. The problems raised by the historical nature of understanding, by the inclusion of one's own historical position in the process of understanding, by the role of historical distance, by the history of reception, have all moved into the center of reflection in modern philosophical hermeneutics since Dilthey, and especially with Gadamer. If we are to outline a contemporary literary hermeneutics, we will have to reexamine traditional philological hermeneutics from this point of view as well.

At the same time as the rise of historical consciousness — and not without a certain causal connection — hermeneutics changed from a set of rules for analyzing what happens in the process of understanding into something of a phenomenological discipline. The ahistorical character of the traditional principles of interpretation is thus understandable, especially since their basic features go back to late antiquity. And yet the ahistorical character of early hermeneutics (from the perspective of what we know today about the historical nature of knowledge) nevertheless merits our consideration, and that is because hermeneutics has been intimately bound up with the problem of historicality from its very beginnings, in both of its dominant orientations.

The first orientation aims to establish what the words in a passage say, to determine the *sensus litteralis*. The second asks in addition what the passage means, what the words, as mere signs, point to. This is the interpretation of the *sensus spiritualis*, allegorical exegesis. Both orientations shaped the beginnings of philological and theological hermeneutics. But how are they related to the problem of historicality?

The task of determining the meaning of a word presented itself very early in Greece with the reading of Homer. Homer's language was no longer immediately intelligible to Athenians of the classical age or to the Alexandrians. Friedrich Blass compares the linguistic gap which separated them from Homer with the distance between us and the *Nibelungenlied*.[7] The phenomenon of linguistic change, the aging of linguistically fixed utterances, thus lies at the source of the impulse to

---

[7] Friedrich Blass, "Hermeneutik und Kritik," in *Handbuch der klassischen Altertums-Wissenschaft in systematischer Darstellung*, ed. Iwan von Müller (Munich, 1892), vol. 1, p. 149.

determine the *sensus litteralis*. The *sensus litteralis* is the *sensus grammaticus*. The hermeneuticist is a translator, a mediator, who uses his linguistic knowledge to make intelligible what is not understood, what is *no longer* understood. He does this by replacing the no longer intelligible word with another one belonging to the current state of the language. Hermeneutic practice thus consisted of overcoming the historical distance to which Homer's work had moved. The object of this activity was not to discover the uniqueness of his work or his language, let alone to reflect on the change itself or on the historical distance. Instead, by replacing with current words those words that had become unintelligible, the historical distance was simply erased. There is more to the aim of determining the *sensus litteralis*, as the *sensus grammaticus*, than a desire to make the unintelligible clear — namely, the desire to draw the canonical text, which Homer was for the Athenians of the classical period and for the Alexandrians, out of its historical remoteness into the present, to make it not only comprehensible but also, as it were, present; to prove its undiminished validity, its right to canonical status.

The impulse to actualize, to annul the historical distance between reader and author, is even clearer in allegorical interpretation than it is in grammatical interpretation — in the theological hermeneutics of Judaism and Christianity as well as in the interpretation of Homer in antiquity. "Allegorical exegesis, or allegoresis, has played a large role in all religions with sacred documents. The aim has been to give fixed formulations a new, contemporary content and thereby to guarantee the authority of the canonical literature."[8] Wolf-Hartmut Friedrich writes about the allegorical interpretation of Homer:

The Homeric epics were canonical for the Greeks; they remained inalienable cultural possessions even when the world in and for which they had arisen no longer existed. Thus in our culture allegoresis developed out of the discussion of Homer; it arose especially out of dissatisfaction with his pronouncements about the gods. The pre-Socratic poet-philosopher Xenophanes protested the slandering of them by Homer and Hesiod, and Plato wanted to drive the poets, as heretics, out of his republic. The answer is allegorical interpretation, which had already been practiced by the Sophists and then by the Cynics, and had been elaborated by the Stoics. By presenting the gods as personifications of cosmic or moral forces, one eliminated everything offensive: the wounding of Aphrodite by Diomedes now meant the victory of Greek virtue over

8 "Allegorie," in *Die Religion in Geschichte und Gegenwart*, vol. 1, col. 238.

barbarian unreason, her adultery with Ares meant a reconciliation of opposing life forces. [...] In the second century before Christ, the stoically inclined philologist Crates of Pergamum believed he could find all the scientific knowledge of his time already contained in Homer.[9]

Thus, to add a few more examples to those Friedrich gives for the interpretation of gods and heroes as personifications, Agamemnon is interpreted as the ether, Achilles as the sun, Helen as the earth, Paris as the air, Hector as the moon; or Demeter as the liver, Dionysus as the spleen, Apollo as the gall bladder. The fruitful identification of the god Cronus with time (*chronos*) also belongs in this context.[10] The allegoresis of the Stoics, who claimed that the notions of the day had been anticipated and prefigured in allegorical disguise by Homer, became the methodological model for the allegorical exegesis of the Old Testament and later also the New Testament. In the second century of the Christian era, for example, the Rabbi Akiba interpreted the Song of Songs, which according to the *sensus litteralis* could not serve as a religious text, as the love song of Israel and Jehovah. The connection between Jewish and Greek allegoresis is clearer still in Philo of Alexandria, who attempted through allegorical interpretation to assimilate the Old Testament to the philosophical mysticism of his time, just as Crates of Pergamum had sought to raise Homer to the level of the natural sciences of his day. Then in Christianity allegorical interpretation of the Old Testament assumes a new function: it proceeds in the light of the New Testament. Early evidence of this sort of allegoresis may be found in the fourth chapter of Galatians. Paul, with whom interpretation of the Old Testament as a prefiguration of the New (so-called "typological interpretation") originates, writes to the Galatians, whom he wants to convert:

Tell me now, you who are so anxious to be under law, will you not listen to what the Law says? It is written there that Abraham had two sons, one by his slave and the other by his free-born wife. The slave-woman's son was born in the course of nature, the free woman's through God's promise. This is an allegory. The two women stand for the two covenants. The one bearing children into slavery is the covenant that comes from Mount Sinai: that is Hagar. Sinai is a mountain in Arabia and it represents the Jerusalem of today, for she and her children are in slavery. But the heavenly Jerusalem is the free woman; she is our mother. For Scripture says, "Rejoice, o barren woman who

---

[9] Wolf-Hartmut Friedrich, "Allegorische Interpretation," in *Fischer Lexikon. Literatur*, ed. Wolf-Hartmut Friedrich and Walter Killy (Frankfurt am Main, 1965), vol. 2, pt. 1, p. 19.   [10] Cf. Blass, "Hermeneutik und Kritik," p. 151.

never bore child; break into a shout of joy, you who never knew a mother's pangs; for the deserted wife shall have more children than she who lives with the husband."

And you, my brothers, like Isaac, are children of God's promise. But just as in those days the natural-born son persecuted the spiritual son, so it is today. But what does Scripture say, "Drive out the slave-woman and her son, for the son of the slave shall not share the inheritance with the free woman's son." You see, then, my brothers, we are no slave-woman's children; our mother is the free woman.[11]

The example is especially suggestive because it presents two figures of the Old Testament as personifications of the Old and New Testaments. The connection between the two, which allegorical interpretation tries to demonstrate, is brought into the Old Testament as an allegorical meaning. At the same time, this example is linked to the interpretation that sees in Abraham's readiness to sacrifice Isaac a prefiguration of God's sacrifice of Christ.

We must not overlook the fact that typological interpretation, in contrast to the Homeric allegoresis of the Stoics, does not so much eliminate historical distance as sublate [*aufheben*] it in the concept of prefiguration, in the difference between promise and fulfillment. The distance is sublated in both senses of the word, because the temporal slope is on the one hand preserved as the difference between promise and fulfillment, while at the same time it is leveled in the preestablished harmony between the Old and New Testaments.

These few examples should suffice to give an idea of the twofold intention that stands at the origin of hermeneutics, along with its motivation: to sublate or, alternatively, to eliminate the historical distance between text and reader. The history of hermeneutics can be understood not only as the orderly course depicted by Dilthey, but with at least equal validity as a series of confrontations between these two orientations. For despite their shared tendency to leap over historical distance, the two modes of interpretation, the grammatical and the allegorical, are opposed to each other. They rely on contrary procedures to solve the problem of the aging of texts, of their becoming unintelligible or obsolete. Grammatical interpretation focuses on what was once meant and wants to preserve this either by replacing the linguistic expression (technically speaking, the sign) that has become historically alien with a new one or by glossing it, accompanying and explaining it with a new expression. Allegorical

[11] Galatians 4: 21–31. Tr. Oxford New English Bible.

interpretation, on the other hand, begins with the sign that has become alien; it gives the sign a new meaning derived not from the conceptual world of the text but from that of the interpreter. It does not have to call the *sensus litteralis* into question in the process because it is based on the possibility of manifold textual meaning. By contrast, grammatical interpretation — which precedes allegorical interpretation historically and thus is not in the first instance to be understood as a counterposition or a critique of it — developed out of the desire to keep that which was once meant from being dragged into the maelstrom of historical change and in this way to maintain it in its identity. The first significant confrontation between these two orientations occurred in patristic hermeneutics, between the Alexandrian and the Antioch schools of theology. The most important theoretical document of the allegorical orientation of the Alexandrians is the fourth book of the *Peri archōn* [*On First Principles*], Origen's dogmatic work from the first half of the third century after Christ:

[T]he way that seems to us right for understanding the Scriptures and seeking their meaning is such that we are taught what sort of understanding we should have of it by no less than Scripture itself. We have found in Proverbs some such instruction for the examination of divine Scripture given by Solomon. He says, "For your part describe them to yourself threefold in admonition and knowledge, that you may answer words of truth to those who question you" (Prov. 22:20–21 LXX). Therefore, a person ought to describe threefold in his soul the meaning of divine letters, that is, so that the simple may be edified by, so to speak, the body of the Scriptures; for that is what we call the ordinary and narrative meaning. But if any have begun to make some progress and can contemplate something more fully, they should be edified by the soul of Scripture. And those who are perfect are like those concerning whom the Apostle says, "Yet among the perfect we do impart wisdom, although it is not a wisdom of this world or of the rulers of this world, who are doomed to pass away. But we impart a secret and hidden wisdom of God, which God decreed before the ages for our glorification" (1 Cor. 2:6–7). Such people should be edified by that spiritual Law (cf. Rom. 7:14) which has a shadow of the good things to come (cf. Heb. 10:1), edified as by the spirit of Scripture. Thus, just as a human being is said to be made up of body, soul, and spirit, so also is sacred Scripture, which has been granted by God's gracious dispensation for man's salvation.[12]

With the last sentence we have what is considered Origen's achievement, which goes far beyond the traditional conception of

---

[12] Origen, *An Exhortation to Martyrdom, Prayer, and Selected Works*, tr. and intro. Rowan A. Greer (New York, 1979), p. 182.

allegoresis. Since the doctrine of threefold textual meaning – the somatic (historical-grammatical), the psychic (moral), and the pneumatic (allegorical-mystical) – corresponds to the trichotomy of Origen's anthropology and ontology, allegoresis, as Ebeling puts it, "does not appear as an arbitrary reinterpretation, but seems to be anchored in the essence of the matter that is actually at issue."[13] The Antioch school of theology does not derive from Alexandrian Platonism, as Origen's theology does, but goes back to the Alexandrian school of philology that is based on the *Rhetoric* of Aristotle. The theologians of Antioch practiced historical-grammatical exegesis and rejected allegoresis, although they did retain the typological interpretation of the Old Testament, that is, its relation to the New Testament. The lost hermeneutic program of Theodorus (from the fourth or fifth century) was called *Contra allegoricos* (it was probably identical with his fragmentary *Liber de allegoria et historia contra Origenem*).

The second decisive confrontation between the two modes of interpretation came during the Reformation, in its battle against the Scholastic doctrine of manifold textual meaning, which had decisively shaped medieval hermeneutics. Late medieval Humanism, in re-actualizing the grammatical tendency which goes back to Aristotle, is extremely important in this battle: the cultivation of biblical languages, editions of texts, and the production of philological commentaries strengthened the position of the adherents of the *sensus litteralis*. Luther is relying on the literal sense when he proclaims the "scriptural principle"[14] which asserts the clarity of Scripture: it interprets itself and needs no external authority for interpretation, such as the church.

These remarks should suffice to indicate the extent to which the opposition between grammatical and allegorical interpretation informs the history of hermeneutics. But it should have become equally clear that the history of hermeneutics is not simply an internal dialectic between these two positions, that, to the contrary, history itself has been at work in the confrontation between the two modes of interpretation. The dawning of the modern age, the change in man's relationship to reality, which manifested itself differently in every

---

[13] Ebeling, "Hermeneutik," p. 247.
[14] See Karl Holl, "Luthers Bedeutung für den Fortschritt der Auslegungskunst," in Holl, *Gesammelte Aufsätze zur Kirchengeschichte*, 6th edn. (Tübingen, 1932), vol. 1, pp. 544–82.

domain (a famous example is the introduction of the third dimension in painting), led in theological hermeneutics to the victory of the principle of grammatical interpretation over allegorical interpretation.

Yet the two tendencies' entanglement with history is immensely more complex than might appear from this textbook example. Not only is the balance of power between them historically conditioned; allegorical interpretation is itself necessarily historical: in shifting a text from another era onto its own historical horizon, allegorical interpretation gives the text an historical index belonging not to the text's originators but its interpreters. Thus we can trace history even within allegoresis. Historical-grammatical interpretation, on the other hand, with its insistence on what was originally meant, which is not to be replaced but to be communicated through translation or commentary, exhibits a certain constancy. Here history seems to be reduced to the gradual refinement of the tools of philological inquiry and to the growth of scholarly literature and knowledge – to the progress of philology as a positivistic discipline. But grammatical-historical interpretation is also subject to historical change, in two ways. On the one hand, the independence from the interpreter's own historical standpoint that is supposed to characterize interpretation of the *sensus litteralis* over against allegoresis is one of intent only, not of practice. Analysis of the interpretive element which is inherent even in positivistic research belongs among the current tasks of hermeneutics. Even if interpreters of the historical-grammatical tendency do not want to be influenced by their own historical standpoint in establishing the *sensus litteralis*, their insistence on the *sensus litteralis* is in turn an historical datum. One's own historical standpoint can easily creep even into philological research: it is, first of all, a factor in deciding whether a passage seems intelligible or unintelligible, that is, in need of improvement; and second, should an emendation, a correction, seem necessary, one's own standpoint affects one's conjecture as to the proper meaning. Not only is the choice of one rather than another possible conjecture already interpretation; which of the possible conjectures occur to the philologist and which do not is a function of his historical horizon.

But there is still another way in which grammatical-historical interpretation is subject to historical change. The orientation toward historical meaning changes with altering conceptions of history. It is not simply that this orientation cannot be the same for the philologist who lived after the rise of historical consciousness in the second half of the eighteenth century and its entrenchment in the Positivism of the nineteenth as it was for the Athenians or Alexandrians, or for the Florentines of the time of Humanism. What Gadamer in *Truth and Method* terms the aporias of historicism[15] have called into question the very basis of grammatical-historical interpretation. Once it has become doubtful that we can learn how things really were in the past, the notion that we are in a position to determine how something was once meant is no less doubtful. The hermeneutics of our time is defined by this shattering of traditional philology, a philology that was historical and thus fancied itself to be independent of its own historical standpoint – a belief that went unchallenged by its practitioners and even seduced them to still greater self-confidence. This shows up especially clearly in the concept of effective-history [*Wirkungsgeschichte*] which has been appropriated for interpretation by Benjamin, but also by Gadamer and, in contemporary literary studies, by, for example, Hans Robert Jauß – in each instance in a very different form.[16] The opinion of a colleague from Classics on a brochure which is strongly influenced by the Critical Theory developed in the thirties, especially by Max Horkheimer, represents another document in this discussion – not a very glorious one, but current.[17]

The method underlying an introduction to literary hermeneutics such as we are attempting here follows from an answer to the question whether a literary hermeneutics exists today. The foregoing reflections and historical digressions show that, and why, we do not today have

---

[15] Hans-Georg Gadamer, *Truth and Method*, 2nd rev. edn., tr. Joel Weinsheimer and Donald G. Marshall (New York, 1989), pp. 218ff.

[16] See Walter Benjamin, "The Task of the Translator," in Benjamin, *Illuminations*, tr. Harry Zohn, ed., intro. Hannah Arendt (New York, 1969), pp. 69–82; the "Epistemo-Critical Prologue" to Benjamin's *The Origin of German Tragic Drama*, tr. John Osborne, intro. George Steiner (London, 1985), pp. 27–56; "Literaturgeschichte und Literaturwissenschaft," in Benjamin, *Gesammelte Schriften*, vol. 3, ed. Hella Tiedemann-Bartels (Frankfurt am Main, 1972), pp. 283–90; "Eduard Fuchs, der Sammler und der Historiker," in Benjamin, *Gesammelte Schriften*, vol. 2, pt. 2, ed. Rolf Tiedemann and Hermann Schweppenhäuser (Frankfurt am Main, 1977), pp. 465–505; "Theses on the Philosophy of History," in Benjamin, *Illuminations*, pp. 253–64; Gadamer, *Truth and Method*, pp. 300–306; Hans Robert Jauß, "Literary History as a Challenge to Literary Theory," in Jauß, *Toward an Aesthetic of Reception*, tr. Timothy Bahti, intro. Paul de Man (Minneapolis, 1982), pp. 3–45.

[17] For Szondi's position in this controversy, see Peter Szondi, *Über eine "Freie (d.h. freie) Universität". Stellungnahmen eines Philologen* (Frankfurt am Main, 1973), pp. 68–87.

a literary hermeneutics in the sense of a material theory of the interpretation of literary texts (that is, a theory that culminates in practice). At the same time we have become aware of the manifold historical implications of hermeneutics. Two things above all follow from this. We cannot simply fill the gap left by the missing literary hermeneutics of our time with the philological hermeneutics that has been handed down from earlier centuries: first, because philological hermeneutics, contrary to its aims, has historical premises; second, because by "literary hermeneutics" we mean a theory of interpretation which, while certainly not unphilological, will reconcile philology with aesthetics. It must, therefore, build on our contemporary understanding of art and so, to that extent, will be historically conditioned and not timeless or universally valid. For this introduction, then, a systematic method of proceeding is just as poorly suited as an historical presentation. The introduction should neither restrict itself to following the historical development of hermeneutics, nor should it ignore that development and try to draft a contemporary hermeneutics *ex nihilo*; for only in a critical examination of earlier theories of hermeneutics is the possibility given us of becoming conscious of the historicality not only of those theories but also of the theory which is to be developed. Thus, the path which recommends itself is a combination of the historical and systematic methods: a critical interrogation of the history of hermeneutics with an eye to a future system that one day will, for its part, appear as historical. Not only practical considerations, of time and competence, but also the logic of the matter at hand dictate that we restrict ourselves to the hermeneutics of those eras which still condition our own: the Enlightenment, the late eighteenth and early nineteenth centuries. In what follows we shall therefore ignore the theories of interpretation of ancient and medieval times as well as the hermeneutics of Humanism and of the Reformation, the main work of which is the *Clavis scripturae sacrae* of Flacius (1567).

Chladenius, I

In the year 1742 there appeared in Leipzig a book 600 pages in length and divided into 753 paragraphs: I mean Johann Martin Chladenius' *Einleitung zur richtigen Auslegung vernünfftiger Reden und Schrifften [Introduction to the Correct Interpretation of Rational Speech and Writing]*. Chladenius lived from 1710 to 1759 and was active in Wittenberg, Leipzig, Coburg, and Erlangen. In addition to philosophical and theological works, he published an *Allgemeine Geschichtswissenschaft [General Historiography]* ten years after the *Einleitung*. If we begin a presentation of literary (that is, specifically not theological or legal) hermeneutics in the eighteenth and nineteenth centuries with Chladenius, we must mention at the outset that he and his hermeneutic work were long forgotten, and are still virtually unknown today. His name appears in none of the long encyclopedia articles on the topic; and even Joachim Wach, who, as far as I can tell, was the first to call attention to Chladenius' hermeneutics again, treated only the *Allgemeine Geschichtswissenschaft* in the first volume (1926) of his three-volume *Geschichte der hermeneutischen Theorie im 19. Jahrhundert: das Verstehen [History of Hermeneutic Theory in the 19th Century: Understanding]*.[1] Not until 1933, in the third volume of his work, did Wach mention and briefly discuss the *Einleitung*. Prior to Wach a few works on historiography referred to Chladenius. For instance, Bernheim, in his *Lehrbuch der historischen Methode und der Geschichtsphilosophie [Treatise on Historical Method and the Philosophy of History]* (1889), said that Chladenius was the first to "try to define in greater detail the relationship of historical method to general epistemology and to logic"[2] –

---

[1] Joachim Wach, *Das Verstehen. Grundzüge einer Geschichte der hermeneutischen Theorie im 19. Jahrhundert*, 3 vols. (Tübingen, 1926–33.; rpt. Hildesheim, 1966), vol. 1, p. 27, n. 2.

[2] Ernst Bernheim, *Lehrbuch der historischen Methode und der Geschichtsphilosophie. Mit Nachweis der wichtigsten Quellen und Hilfsmittel zum Studium der Geschichte*, 5th and 6th rev. and exp. edn. (Leipzig, 1908), p. 183.

something no one after him tried again for a long time. The German literary scholar Rudolf Unger also mentioned Chladenius in 1923 in an "historiographical sketch" entitled "Zur Entwicklung des Problems der historischen Objektivität bis Hegel" ["On the Development of the Problem of Historical Objectivity up to Hegel"].[3]

In contrast to his predecessors, Wach knew not only the *Allgemeine Geschichtswissenschaft* of Chladenius, but also his *Einleitung*, and he pointed out that the *Allgemeine Geschichtswissenschaft* was actually a reworking of the eighth chapter of the *Einleitung*, entitled "Von Auslegung historischer Nachrichten und Bücher" ["On the Interpretation of Historical Accounts and Books"].[4] Although Wach was familiar with the general hermeneutic framework of Chladenius' ideas on the relativity of historical knowledge, the section on Chladenius in his third volume[5] remains wholly under the aegis of this latter, narrower question and the answer put forward in Chladenius' theory of the "point of view" [*Sehe-Punckt*]. I do not call attention to the one-sidedness of Wach's presentation of Chladenius' hermeneutics in order to criticize it. Wach mentions Chladenius in the context of historiography from Ranke to Positivism. It was therefore natural for him to consider Chladenius as a precursor of those historiographers who were concerned with the problem of the objectivity of historical knowledge and who, from Droysen to Dilthey, exerted a decisive influence on the later development of hermeneutics.[6] We cannot overlook the theory of the "point of view," but it is certainly not the only remarkable feature of Chladenius' work. A detailed discussion of his voluminous book is beyond the scope of our study; but because it is important not only to become aware of specific hermeneutic problems, but to get an idea as well of the nature and goals of hermeneutic systems as such, we must first consider this work as a whole.

Chladenius' subject, as the title announces, is the "correct interpretation of rational speech and writing." The two adjectives, which show the spirit of the eighteenth century (compare the terse title in common use previously, *ars interpretandi*), have a definite

---

[3] Rudolf Unger, *Gesammelte Studien*, vol. 1: *Aufsätze zur Prinzipienlehre der Literaturgeschichte* (Berlin, 1929; rpt. Darmstadt, 1966), pp. 98–100.
[4] Wach, *Das Verstehen*, vol. 3, p. 26, n. 2.   [5] Ibid., pp. 23–32.
[6] Szondi had intended to discuss the relationship between objectivity and hermeneutics in the second part of his course, which was not given. See translator's preface, above, p. xxvi.

function which is itself in need of interpretation. The word "rational" indicates the sort of speech and writing we will be taught to interpret; the word "correct" refers less to the claim than to the aim of such interpretation. By not specifying any one type of text as the object of interpretation, Chladenius goes beyond traditional hermeneuticists, who had dedicated themselves to the Scriptures or the *corpus juris* or the writings of antiquity. He rejects traditional hermeneutic specialization in favor of a general theory of interpretation, something that had not existed before the eighteenth century. But Chladenius' theory of interpretation has limits which clearly differentiate it from later contributions, from Schleiermacher to Gadamer and Betti. The latter are concerned with a theory of understanding in which, since Schleiermacher, the differences among the writings to be understood have become progressively less relevant. Chladenius, however, does not ask how one understands, but how one interprets something correctly — which is a question that arises only when correct understanding cannot be vouchsafed, when a passage is obscure. The two terms "correct" and "rational," even before their background is examined, reveal Chladenius' place in the history of hermeneutics: he takes hermeneutics out of a long period of specialization during which it treated only one particular area; but he brings about this unification neither at the expense of the concrete problems with which interpretation must deal nor at the expense of the real diversity of the texts to be interpreted, which only a philosophical-psychological theory of understanding could ignore. In saying this I have already suggested why Chladenius' work holds particular interest for us: it is general enough to encompass even those problems which a contemporary literary hermeneutics would view as constitutive, however differently it would handle them; but it is also empirical, which means it is specific enough not to ignore individual problems for the sake of concentrating on an act of understanding.

What is meant by the "interpretation of rational speech and writing"? In the Preface we read:

... the doctrines set forth in the book present a general art of interpretation, that is, a discipline which is valid for all kinds of books and which is adequate to all kinds of books. An exception must be made, however, in the case of the Scriptures. I view the interpretation of this holy and divine book as a *chef d'œuvre* and a masterpiece of interpretation, in which one must employ not only all the tools of the philosophical and general art of interpretation, but also other special rules. The Scriptures contain mysteries, so an interpreter has to interpret mysterious passages. But everyone is certain to agree with me that it is one thing to elucidate passages which contain something discovered by human wit and reason, and something else again to elucidate passages which contain things transcending reason. Everyone will at least have to admit that one has to supplement the rules for interpreting the books of mortals with all sorts of annotation and commentary if they are to be applied directly to a book of divine origin and containing divine wisdom. These notes, qualifications, and comments belong to exegetical theology, which has been treated quite thoroughly by various divines of our church. The philosophical art of interpretation should therefore be considered only as a preparation, albeit a very useful one, for the interpretation of the Scriptures; it does not contain everything that it is necessary to know and observe therein.[a]

The word "rational," according to this passage, not only indicates that we are to be instructed in a general hermeneutics or, as Chladenius also says, a philosophical hermeneutics, and not a specialized (say, legal or historical) hermeneutics; at the same time the word also establishes the limits of this discipline. The Scriptures, as revealed truth, do not belong to the body of rational literature. Chladenius thus retains the traditional distinction between *hermeneutica sacra* and *profana*. But this is not an absolute difference. Since the time of Humanism and the Reformation, the principles of secular hermeneutics – that is, the philological hermeneutics developed for classical texts – have become increasingly relevant to biblical hermeneutics. Chladenius makes this point when he describes the general art of interpretation, which is his subject, as preparation for the interpretation of the Scriptures. Its rules are not completely inadequate to the Scriptures, but they must be supplemented with rules which take into account the Scriptures' revelatory nature. The distinction which Chladenius respects between *hermeneutica sacra* and *profana* is closely related to his demand that the task and the rules of hermeneutics be made dependent on the nature or genre of the text to be interpreted, even in the case of the general art of interpretation which he is outlining.

There is a definite tension between the postulate of a general hermeneutics which purports to be valid for all writings, or at least for all rational writings (that is, those of human origin), and such content-specificity [*Inhaltsbezogenheit*]. Fifteen years after Chladenius, Georg

---

[a] Johann Martin Chladenius, *Einleitung zur richtigen Auslegung vernünfftiger Reden und Schrifften*, ed. and intro. Lutz Geldsetzer (Leipzig, 1742; rpt. Düsseldorf, 1962), b4f. Subsequent references will appear in the text.

Friedrich Meier published his *Versuch einer allgemeinen Auslegungskunst* [*Toward a General Theory of Interpretation*].[7] As Dilthey points out in his "Development of Hermeneutics,"[8] this work united classical and biblical hermeneutics and developed a general semiology which of necessity abstracted from the specific text to be interpreted. The internal antinomy which had characterized Chladenius' system disappeared in this later work; but we will want to ask with respect to a contemporary literary hermeneutics whether this represents progress – whether the content-specificity of hermeneutics can or should be relinquished. Of course, there are problems associated with a hermeneutics that is content-specific, inasmuch as it presupposes that the classification of a text, which is supposed to dictate the rules for its interpretation, is not determined through interpretation but is known in advance. This is indisputably the case when it is a matter of distinguishing, say, legal from historical writing; but problems already arise with the distinction between historical works and works of imaginative literature. To what extent these problems – which Chladenius may or may not have been aware of – are reflected in his system, even though it distinguishes only a few genres, will need to be explored, as will the question of content-specificity with regard to the various kinds of imaginative literature.

Chladenius formulates the postulate of content-specificity in his Preface:

Interpretation depends on the nature of the subject matter which is presented in a book or passage. One will always have to replace what the mere words of a passage cannot effect for the reader who brings to the book no other knowledge than that of the language, and bring the reader to the point where he can understand the passage. Now one kind of knowledge is presupposed for a dogmatic passage, another for an historical passage, another for a dry dogmatic or historical passage, another for a meaning-full [*sinnreich*] dogmatic or historical passage, another for a law, another for a wish or a promise; hence an interpreter has a different task with every type of passage, depending on the nature of its content. Thus it is also necessary in the art of interpretation to go through all types of passages, according to their content, and to indicate what each one presupposes in the way of knowledge; in this way the

[7] Georg Friedrich Meier, *Versuch einer allgemeinen Auslegungskunst*, ed. and intro. Lutz Geldsetzer (Halle, 1757; rpt. Düsseldorf, 1965). Subsequent references are given in the text.
[8] Dilthey, "The Development of Hermeneutics," p. 255. Cf. Chapters 6 and 7 below.

causes of obscurity which can arise in each type of passage, as well as the means of eliminating them, will become apparent by themselves.   (b2)

It is quite clear that the postulate of content-specificity here is derived from a particular understanding of the hermeneutic task and – prior to this – from a certain understanding of the structure of a text, of what a passage is and of what makes it obscure. What we just called an inherent tension in Chladenius' system between content-specificity and the presumption of universal validity may be located more exactly at the point where the concept of the passage, of its possible obscurity and the interpretation necessitated by this obscurity, passes over into the concept of a special hermeneutics – dogmatic, historical, legal. We may surmise that Chladenius' plan to present a "general art of interpretation, that is, a discipline appropriate to all kinds of books" (b4), is compatible with his aforementioned requirement that interpretation begin with a consideration of the nature of the subject matter presented in the book to be interpreted only because his hermeneutics is based on a certain conception of the text: in his view it is not the nature of a particular passage itself which will vary, according to the subject matter, but only its interpretation. That is, any interpretation has to do justice less to the passage than to the subject matter presented in the passage. The passage itself is of lesser importance because, as Chaldenius understands it, its structure remains the same despite variations in the subject matter and the consequent variation in interpretation.

This problem is of fundamental importance, as we shall see. It also explains why Chladenius can call his work a general art of interpretation even though it deals with only two kinds of speech and writing: (1) "historical accounts and books" and (2) "universal truths and treatises."[9] What is missing, then, is not only theological hermeneutics but also legal and – a crucial omission for our purposes – philological or literary hermeneutics. The Preface addresses this problem:

[I am] presenting at this time only the elements of the whole art of interpretation and will not go beyond historical and dogmatic books. But there are still other types of books and passages worthy of interpretation. Foremost among them are laws, which, along with commands, promises, contracts, and other dispositions, can be neatly classified under the general concept of intentions. [...] There is yet another type of book which must be

[9] Chladenius, *Einleitung*, Chapters 8 (pp. 181–370) and 9 (pp. 371–496).

examined more closely in discussing the art of interpretation, and that is the wise or meaning-full [*sinnreich*] book, foremost among which are works of literature [*poetische Bücher*]. Inasmuch as a special way of thinking rules in these books, such that they seem to contain a special theory of reason, so is their interpretation quite different from wholly dogmatic or merely historical books. I intend to treat this important chapter in the art of interpretation [...].

(b3)

It seems that this continuation never appeared, and the *Allgemeine Geschichtswissenschaft*, which Chladenius published ten years after the *Einleitung*, shows that the priority given to historical writings over literary writings in the earlier work coincides with a special interest of his. This is all the more regrettable since his mention of a "special theory of reason" contained in literary works, which implies the notion of a specifically literary logic, not only represents an exceptionally bold thought for the first half of the eighteenth century, but is all the more relevant to our understanding of literature today, inasmuch as such a literary logic is still a desideratum, and exists at best in rudimentary form. Chladenius' work already contains such rudiments, and that is one reason why it deserves our close attention here. Moreover, Chladenius does not ignore literature completely, despite restricting himself to historical and dogmatic works, because the phenomenon of the meaning-full [*des Sinnreichen*], which he appears to consider constitutive of literature, also plays a role in historical and dogmatic works. As mentioned earlier, in deriving the necessary differences in interpretation, Chladenius distinguishes between dry dogmatic, dry historical, meaning-full dogmatic, and meaning-full historical passages. The fact, then, that the concept of the "point of view" – that is, of historical situatedness [*Standortgebundenheit*] – will not be at the center of our concern, as it was in Wach, can now be formulated in a positive way: because the rudiments of a literary hermeneutics, which, as Chladenius sees it, presupposes a literary logic, are contained in his treatment of the meaning-full passages of historical and dogmatic books, we shall have to devote our attention to these – or in other words to the theory of metaphor which Chladenius develops.

First, however, we must explore Chladenius' definition of interpretation and the specification of the task of interpretation which follows from that definition. In the Preface we read the following, which serves as a point of departure for the above-cited passage on content-specificity:

Chapter 2

Take a commentary and eliminate everything in it which has been contributed by criticism and philology. What remains will be the elucidation of passages which one suspected would be encountered by readers without sufficient insight to understand them, and one provides these readers with the concepts and knowledge which they might lack. Interpretation is thus nothing other than the teaching of those concepts which are necessary for complete understanding of a passage. (b1f.)

Chladenius was aware that this definition of interpretation deviated from the traditional one. Usually, he continues, it is said that interpretation "is the same as indicating the true understanding of a passage" (b2). This concept of interpretation is not wrong, he maintains, but his own definition provides "a sounder basis for a philosophical theory of interpretation, and makes it much clearer what an interpreter should do with any type of obscure passage" (b2). It would be idle to ask whether Chladenius is right or wrong. Instead, we must ask what notion of *understanding*, that is, of the meaning of a passage, and what idea of its possible obscurity lead to his definition of interpretation as the teaching of concepts which are necessary for complete understanding of a passage, but which the reader might lack.

Incidentally, it is no coincidence that what we call the "meaning" of a word or passage as well as what we call our "understanding" [*Verstehen*; *Verständnis*] are both called "understanding" [*Verstand*] by Chladenius. As later in Hegel's use of the word "concept" [*Begriff*], the subjective and the objective converge in the word "understanding." But unlike Hegel, Chladenius uses the term with a kind of naive immediacy, which is the reason that, despite isolated insights that are astonishingly bold for the eighteenth century and astonishingly relevant today, Chladenius' hermeneutics as a whole is in no respect adequate to the contemporary state of knowledge.

This becomes apparent when he enumerates the various kinds of obscurity in a passage in order to make clear which kind of obscurity interpretation treats. Obscurity may arise

sometimes from a corrupt passage; and this obscurity is removed by a critic when he emends and restores the text. Or it arises from inadequate knowledge of the language in which the book is written; and this obscurity must be removed by a grammarian or philologist. Or the words are themselves ambiguously arranged; this obscurity cannot be removed by any properly grounded means. None of this is the concern of the interpreter or, consequently, of the art of interpretation. But it frequently occurs that one also fails to understand passages which have none of these obscurities. [...]

21

Closer investigation shows that this obscurity arises because the mere words and sentences are not always able to evoke in the reader the concept which the author has associated with them, and that knowledge of a language alone does not enable us to understand all books and passages written in it. A thought which is to be called forth in the reader by words often presupposes other concepts without which it is incomprehensible; therefore, if the reader lacks these prior concepts, the words cannot have the effect or occasion the concepts that they would with a reader who is appropriately instructed.

(before b)

Contemporary hermeneutics must go beyond the conception formulated here in two respects. When Chladenius assigns the first two types of obscurity, which arise either from a corrupt text or from inadequate linguistic knowledge, to the domain of the textual critic or the grammarian and denies that they belong to the hermeneuticist's area of competence, he is following a tradition which, even in the nineteenth and twentieth centuries, regards hermeneutics and textual criticism as neighboring but independent disciplines. In opposition to this view, one would need to show that the establishment of a clean text and the clarification of a passage on the basis of the history of a language – the province of textual critic and grammarian – are always interpretation as well; criticism and hermeneutics are interdependent. The conjecture of a textual critic, even the assumption that a conjecture, an intervention in the text, is necessary, cannot be separated from his understanding of the passage, just as the deciphering of a manuscript does not simply precede understanding and ground it, but always occurs along with it – in a process in which understanding and deciphering mutually anticipate, confirm, and correct each other.[10] The case is similar with problems posed by grammar and the history of language. Without knowledge of certain possible constructions and word meanings which are no longer present in contemporary German (let us disregard the problem of foreign languages), many a passage in texts from, say, the eighteenth century is doubtless incomprehensible. But the following example will show that simply knowing the meaning that a word could have had does not guarantee correct understanding of a passage either, hence that the decision as to meaning is always a hermeneutic decision as well.

---

[10] Cf. Szondi, "Interpretationsprobleme," in Szondi, *Einführung in die literarische Hermeneutik. Studienausgabe der Vorlesungen*, vol. 5 (Frankfurt am Main, 1975), pp. 266ff., 306ff.

In Goethe's pastoral play *Die Laune des Verliebten* [*The Lover's Caprice*] of 1767, one reads:

> Der eine nach ihr sieht, sie nach dem andern blickt.
> Denck' ich nur dran, mein Herz möcht' da für Boßheit reißen.[11]
>
> [Someone makes eyes at her, she makes eyes at someone else.
> If I so much as think about it, my heart is torn with malice.]

If we assume that in order to understand a work, one must know the language in which it is written, and therefore that to understand this play, one must know German as it was used in the 1760s and '70s, then for these lines one would have to know that at that time *Boßheit* [malice] could also mean *Ärger* [anger] or *Wut* [rage]. This linguistic information is based on the dictionaries of the time and today can most conveniently be found in Grimm's dictionary.[b] Thus far the passage seems to belong to Chladenius' second type of obscurity, which "arises from inadequate knowledge of the language in which the book is written, and this obscurity must be removed by a grammarian or philologist" (before b). The "interpreter, and hence also the art of interpretation," have nothing to do with such obscurity, according to Chladenius. But we have to ask: (1) whether we are actually dealing with obscurity at all, and (2) whether the information from the historical dictionary really clarifies the meaning of the passage. This passage will not initially be considered obscure, because everybody who reads it will find it comprehensible. Not knowing that *Boßheit* had several meanings in the eighteenth century, one will simply attribute to the word its current univocal meaning. Only upon closer consideration of what is being said in the passage is one liable to ask whether someone would mention, and thereby admit, his own malice. But that is already a question of interpretation, and whether or not one accepts such a confession will depend on the character of the figure, on the style of the play, and on the place of the passage in the play (is it a monologue or a dialogue, if a dialogue, with whom?). The lines from the opening monologue of the future Richard III, this confession of malice and villainy –

---

[11] Johann Wolfgang von Goethe, *Gedenkausgabe der Werke, Briefe und Gespräche*, vol. 4: *Der junge Goethe*, ed. E. Beutler (Zurich, 1953), p. 34.

[b] The *Deutsches Wörterbuch*, German equivalent of the *Oxford English Dictionary*, begun in 1852 by the brothers Jakob and Wilhelm Grimm and not completed until 1960.

... since I cannot prove a lover,
To entertain these fair well-spoken days,
I am determined to prove a villain,
And hate the idle pleasures of these days.[12]

– are they conceivable in Goethe's pastoral play, in a rococo atmosphere? Hardly. But this is not the answer of an historian of the language, because in 1760 *Boßheit* could also have meant what it means today; such an answer is the result of interpretation. This in turn means that the obscurity of the passage is not obvious, but instead will be noticed and eliminated only in the course of interpretation. Use of an historical dictionary presupposes that the passage, which is not in itself incomprehensible (Richard III could perfectly well say that malice rends his heart), seem to the reader as if it might have been misunderstood for historical, stylistic reasons. Similarly, the information that the word once also meant "anger" or "rage" can be evaluated only through interpretation, which has to decide whether the one or the other meaning or both meanings of the word are to be assigned to the passage. Strictly speaking, only the second step, the evaluation of historical knowledge through interpretation, is of interest to a hermeneutic theory; the first step is too dependent on accident, that is, on whether one encounters a difficulty on first reading or only on closer consideration, on whether one is aware of the earlier ambiguity of the word or discovers it in a dictionary. I mention this only because Chladenius speaks of the obscurity which arises from insufficient linguistic knowledge and is to be removed by the philologist. However, instead of obscurity, a misunderstanding can arise which can be identified and eliminated only by hermeneutics.

Chladenius lists four types of obscurity, the first two of which are supposed to be the exclusive domain of the textual critic or the grammarian. From the point of view of our contemporary understanding, however, hermeneutics is involved in these cases, too, since the grammarian's information about a passage can only be evaluated in the context of its interpretation, whereas the work of the textual critic, the decision, say, in favor of one reading over another, or a conjecture, always presupposes an understanding of the passage.

Chladenius similarly contests the competence of hermeneutics to

---

[12] William Shakespeare, *Richard III*, ed. J. D. Wilson (Cambridge, 1971), Act I, Scene I, ll. 28–31.

treat his third type of obscurity, that which arises when "words themselves are ambiguously arranged." This obscurity, he says, "cannot be removed by any properly grounded means" (before b). Chladenius discusses this more extensively in §179, in connection with a sketch of the "previous state of hermeneutics" (pp. 96–103). The shortcomings of hermeneutics he attributes to the false demands which have been placed on it. After taking issue with the conflation of textual criticism and hermeneutics, which we have just tried to justify, or at least to demonstrate as interdependent activities, he writes:

> Furthermore, things have been demanded of interpretation which were impossible either in themselves or according to the few rules of interpretation that exist. Interpretation actually takes place only when it is the fault of the reader or listener that one or more passages are not understood. On the other hand, it is impossible to find an interpretation when the words have nothing in themselves through which one could reach a certain or probable understanding. But this is precisely what has been demanded of the interpreter: that he give certain meaning to passages which are essentially obscure and ambiguous. This is quite impossible. [...] It cannot be denied that where no absolutely certain interpretation is possible, there might well be a probable interpretation; but this would be as difficult to formulate in rules as the rational theory of the probable, which is still in a very sorry state, whereas it has been conclusively shown how one can recognize truth with certainty.   (pp. 98f.)

This passage is of great importance because words which are "themselves ambiguously arranged" are a component, if not of all literature, then certainly of one of its possibilities, hermetic literature, with which, understandably, hermeneutics has of late been especially occupied. Latter-day hermeneutics leaves Chladenius behind in two respects. It neither demands that "words" have something "in themselves through which one could reach a certain or probable understanding," nor does it demand of itself that interpretation be codified in rules which need only be applied. It might appear that this normative attitude makes it impossible for Chladenius to do justice to an inherent feature of poetic language. But the passage just cited already contains a hint that Chladenius does not mean to leave things here, and that another, contrary tendency will join the normative, rationalist tendency which his work shares with most of the works of his time. This other tendency sets him apart from his time and may well be the reason he attracted so little attention. It is the allusion to the "rational theory of the probable," which was "still in a very sorry state." As it happens, Chladenius himself published a work in 1748 entitled *Vernünftige Gedanken vom Wahrscheinlichen [Rational Thoughts on the Probable]*. We may surmise, therefore, that despite his postulation of univocality, actual ambiguity did not leave him cold – proof of this is the significance he assigns to the phenomenon of the meaning-full, even in the context of interpreting historical and dogmatic writings. It may be surmised that rationalism here encounters the fascinating spectacle of someone withdrawing from it.

3

Chladenius, II

The word "rational" points to the limitations of the *hermeneutica profana*: it is merely a prolegomenon to the *hermeneutica sacra*. The word "correct," on the other hand, refers to the type of application Chladenius intends for his hermeneutics. Both his definition of understanding [*Verstehen*] – the *raison d'être* of interpretation – and his definition of obscurity – the sole field of action for the hermeneuticist – are limited in a way that must be questioned by contemporary hermeneutics. In the first instance, obscurity is hardly the only occasion for interpretation. Secondly, we must ask whether interpretation should deal only with that type of obscurity that arises from the reader's ignorance of certain information presupposed by a passage, while other types of obscurity either are to be clarified by the critic or the grammarian or are altogether impervious to clarification "by any properly grounded means." It remains to be seen to what extent we are dealing with questions that were already being answered in a fundamentally different way at the end of the eighteenth century – I am thinking, for instance, of the restriction of hermeneutics to "correct" interpretation – and to what extent these are questions which still pose a challenge to literary hermeneutics today.

To assess the originality of Chladenius' theory of interpretation and its significance in the history of hermeneutics, we must familiarize ourselves with the basic concepts and ideas that give content to the structure of meaning and the criteria and methods for interpreting meaning. Interpreting, according to Chladenius, is "nothing other than teaching someone the concepts necessary to understand completely, or learn to understand, a speech or written text" (§169, pp. 92f.). But what does it mean to "understand completely"? "One understands a speech or written text completely when one thinks of all the things which the words can awaken in us in accordance with reason and the rules of our soul" (§155, p. 86). This definition is one of the most fruitful in all of Chladenius' system. Two aspects in particular should be noted here in brief: Chladenius defines understanding without recourse to the author or authorial intention. For him understanding a speech or written text is evidently different from imagining "what the writer thought with the words" (§156, p. 86). Chladenius must have anticipated his readers' astonishment, for in the same paragraph he explains why this is so:

Understanding a speech or written text completely and understanding the speaker or writer completely ought, indeed, to be one and the same thing. [...] However, because people cannot survey the whole, their words, speech, and writings can mean things they themselves did not intend to say or write. It follows that in trying to understand their writings one can with good reason think of things which did not occur to the authors. (§156, pp. 86f.)

There is also the opposite situation, in which an author imagines that he has expressed his view so as to be completely understood, but "his words do not supply us with all we would need to be able to comprehend his meaning fully" (§156, p. 87). Only the first case is relevant epistemologically, because in the second we are dealing with an accidental failure on the part of the author. Chladenius states explicity that, on the other hand, where the reader understands not less but more than the author himself, we are not necessarily dealing with a failure or mistake on the part of the reader: one could "with good reason" (§156, p. 87) imagine more than the author himself thought in many a passage. The fact that Chladenius seems to abstract in this way from the author's intention and that he attributes a kind of autonomous existence to words gives his hermeneutic theory a very modern ring. We must therefore inquire all the more into how he was able to reconcile such views with the rationalistic framework of his thinking.

If one reads the arguments in his closing chapter, entitled "Von den allgemeinen Eigenschafften der Auslegung" ["On the General Characteristics of Interpretation"] (pp. 497–600), one gets the impression that Chladenius himself sensed he had ventured too far in this matter, that he wished to assert the identity of interpreted and intended meaning in spite of his insight that the objective meaning [*Sinn*] of a passage may include more than its author intended. Yet the definition of "complete understanding" cited above contains a critical element which is meant to counter the danger that the reader's associations will take over and arbitrarily assign meanings to a passage, without any possibility of objective verification, as soon as authorial intention is eliminated as a criterion of interpretation. That Chladenius had nothing of the sort in mind is indicated by his qualifying statement that in order to understand a passage completely, one ought to "think of all the things which the words can awaken in us in accordance with reason and the rules of our soul" (§155, p. 86). In short, association follows reason and the rules of the soul. The normative force which is denied to authorial intention is assigned to logic and psychology, a psychology which, unlike today's, is itself normative. Thus, the solution to the problem of how doing away with intention as a touchstone in interpretation is to be reconciled with rationalism is provided by a rationalist psychology of reception [*Rezeptionspsychologie*], which shapes Chladenius' hermeneutics as much as the aesthetics of effect [*Wirkungsästhetik*] did the poetics of his contemporaries. Corresponding to the process of "completely understanding" [*Vollkommen-Verstehen*] a passage is its "complete sense" [*vollkommener Verstand*]. Chladenius writes:

The complete sense [consists of] numerous concepts which can be awakened by the passage in question. These concepts fall into three categories [...]. First of all, we discover in a passage a particular concept which arises from the passage simply as a result of our attentiveness when we approach the text with the requisite knowledge and background. This type of concept which is brought forth by mere attentiveness to the words of the passage is called the *straightforward sense* [*unmittelbarer Verstand*] by teachers of the art of interpretation. This straightforward sense then gives rise to all kinds of other concepts which are brought forth by the various faculties of the soul, with the exception of the imagination. These concepts are called the *application* [*Anwendung*] *of a passage*, or the *mediated sense* [*mittelbarer Verstand*] *of a passage*, as well as the *conclusions* [*Folgerungen*], because this type of concept usually consists of deductions and logical conclusions. Thirdly, the straightforward sense gives rise to concepts which are brought forth by the imagination, and these are called *digressions* [*Ausschweiffungen*] [...].

(§674, pp. 518f.)

This distinction between the straightforward and mediated senses of a passage carries forward the traditional, theological hermeneutic theory of manifold textual meaning, but modifies it in a critical way, as the terminology itself here indicates. When Chladenius says that the straightforward sense "is brought forth by mere attentiveness to the words of the passage," it is clear that he is referring to the *sensus litteralis*, the literal meaning, which since antiquity has been contrasted with a *sensus spiritualis*. Chladenius' critique begins with this contrast: the straightforward sense is generally set beside the *literal sense* as if it were an equivalent term [i.e., synonym], which, however, it is not. The literal sense is contrasted with the mystical meaning. Therefore, where no mystical sense exists, one cannot speak of the literal sense either. Now, the mystical sense is not present in all texts; nor, therefore, is the literal sense either. But the straightforward sense is present in all texts, regardless of what they are called or what characteristics they have. Therefore, one ought to consider the literal sense only as a particular type of straightforward sense.   (§675, p. 520)

This departure from patristic and medieval hermeneutics has a twofold background: in an earlier paragraph which spoke of the damage "which has been done by ignorance of hermeneutics," Chladenius says that

the sciences based on interpretation have deteriorated so badly – not only philosophy through the embarrassing interpretation of Aristotle, but jurisprudence through the glosses, and theology through the interpretations of the Fathers and the Scholastics – that there appears to be no help for it but simply to throw out all the interpretations and start all over again from the beginning.   (§186, pp. 104f.)

This fresh start began in theological hermeneutics with Luther, who declared the Holy Scripture to be its own interpreter (*sui ipsius interpres*),[1] and therewith rejected allegorical interpretation. To be sure, Chladenius neither proposes restricting interpretation to the *sensus litteralis* nor does he declare the text itself judge of the correctness of an interpretation.[2] As far as may be determined from his *Einleitung*, which, as we have noted, does not deal with theological hermeneutics, he criticizes patristic and Scholastic exegesis not because it assumes the possibility of manifold textual meaning, but because it does not treat such meaning *as* a mere possibility, which the passage in question must in each case confirm, but instead feels licensed to ascribe multiple meanings to every passage. Chladenius' understanding undoubtedly does an injustice to the Scholastic doctrine of the fourfold scriptural meaning. The intention behind the conceptual apparatus *sensus litteralis, sensus allegoricus, sensus tropologicus, sensus anagogicus* was not to oblige the interpreter to ascribe to every passage the three different *sensus spirituales* in addition to the literal sense. Rather, within what one could broadly call allegorical interpretation and in line with

---

[1] See Holl, "Luthers Bedeutung für den Fortschritt der Auslegungskunst," p. 559, n. 4.   [2] See above, pp. 29ff.

Chapter 3

Scholastic *distinguo*, the point was to distinguish and define more clearly various modes of interpretation according to point of view and function.

Implicit in Chladenius's insistence that there may, but need not, be a "mystical sense," and that it is meaningful to speak of a "literal sense" only where it can be contrasted to a mystical one, is a broadening of hermeneutics from a theological to a general exegetic process. Herein lies a second feature of Chladenius' departure from patristic and medieval hermeneutics. The logical consequence of what we have called the postulate of content-specificity is that, according to Chladenius, the type of text and the nature of the passage themselves must decide whether or not we may assume the presence of a mystical sense. The terminology, "straightforward sense" and "mediated sense," and within the latter, "application" and "digression," is conceived in keeping with the goal of a general art of interpretation so as to be valid for all types of speech and writing – although, as Chladenius demonstrates in numerous examples, the individual elements of meaning will vary according to the type of book being interpreted.

To proceed now to a closer specification of these elements of the complete understanding of a passage (or of an entire text), in §677 we read that

the straightforward sense is the one about which the author of the passage and all the readers who comprehend the passage must be in agreement. That is to say, the complete understanding/sense of a passage consists of many concepts. The straightforward sense constitutes one component thereof. However, one can understand a passage even if one does not immediately think of everything that could reasonably be thought of in connection with the passage. Thus it is that a reader can understand a passage even though he does not think certain thoughts which the author had in mind. It follows that the author will not concur with all of those readers who can be said to have understood the passage. However, with regard to the straightforward sense, the author must be in agreement with all of his readers, provided that they have understood him. For since this level of meaning is the result of mere attention to the words of the passage and demands the least amount of attention from the reader, the straightforward sense can remain concealed from no one so long as he has properly prepared himself beforehand. The author, too, must know what the straightforward sense is, as needs no proof. Thus, the straightforward sense is known to both the author and all of those readers who understand him, and it follows that with regard to the straightforward meaning the author is in agreement with all the readers who understand him. (pp. 522f.)

31

This definition should be viewed against the background of Chladenius' insight, cited earlier, that "because people cannot survey the whole, their words, speech, and writings can mean things which they themselves did not intend to say or write," and that therefore "in trying to understand their writings one can with good reason think of things which did not occur to the authors" (§156, pp. 86f.). At this point Chladenius restricts the applicability of his insight: it is not valid for the "straightforward sense," about which author and reader must, on the contrary, agree. In other words, the division of "complete understanding" which Chladenius undertakes, and which up to now could be viewed as a modification of the traditional distinction between *sensus litteralis* and *sensus spiritualis*, proves to be an attempt to resolve the latent crisis of hermeneutics in the Age of Enlightenment. We may speak of a crisis because in the field of hermeneutics the insights of rationalism come into conflict with its postulates. Among the insights which date Chladenius' critical position – a position indebted to no tradition and to no authority save that of reason – is his recognition of the subjective and historical nature of understanding, as presented in his theory of the "point of view" (to which we will turn later on).

Chladenius' insight does not have to do with the subjective arbitrariness and the anachronisms of allegorical interpretation. If this were so, then it would suffice for him to insist upon the grammatical-historical method of interpretation as the only legitimate one. But Chladenius recognizes that there is something subjective in every act of understanding, and that this is necessarily so. Precisely because the hermeneutics of rationalism, in contrast to the apodictic-authoritarian hermeneutics of earlier periods, does recognize an individual component in understanding, it must, if it is to satisfy the postulate of universal validity, delimit this subjective component. What keeps the individual component from expanding and taking over the entire process of understanding in Chladenius' system is his division of "complete understanding" into a straightforward sense and a mediated sense, whereby the "straightforward sense" is removed from the influence of the reader's or interpreter's subjectivity and historicity. It is, so to speak, the stable part, where the author's intention and the reader's understanding coincide. It is surrounded by other, changeable parts which arise in the imagination of the author or the reader and in both cases belong to an understanding of the passage, though there is no guarantee that the two will be identical.

Chladenius distinguishes these elements of meaning, as belonging to "mediated" sense, from the "straightforward" sense. The latter allows him, despite his recognition of the significance of "point of view" and the varying, personal understanding of a passage, to postulate "certainty" of meaning.

It would be premature to begin a critical assessment of Chladenius' theory here, inasmuch as we have yet to examine the complementary concept of the "mediated" sense and its components. The question his theory raises is nevertheless worth mentioning in passing, and that is: Can the meaning of a pasage be split into two parts, as Chladenius proposes? Does the motive for this division – namely, the recognition that understanding depends on the position of the interpreter – admit the possibility of a core of "straightforward sense" beyond all relativity? Should we not pose and solve the problem of the validity of understanding and interpretation *within* the theory of their historical situatedness [*Standortgebundenheit*] rather than try to rescue the traditional criteria of the objectivity of understanding by postulating a "straightforward sense"?

The "mediated sense" of a passage consists of "those concepts or ideas [...] which are brought forth and elicited by the straightforward sense gleaned from a passage" (§683, p. 528). Chladenius also refers to it as the "application." He explains this second component of "complete sense/understanding" as follows:

Because the straightforward sense emerges directly from the words through the simple use of attentiveness, whereas the mediated sense, or application, emerges from the concept gleaned from the words, it follows that the mediated sense of a passage does not have to do with the words of the passage directly, but is dependent upon the use of our various faculties [*Gemüths-Kräffte*], by means of which we bring forth out of the straightforward sense all manner of other concepts and impulses. (§684, p. 529).

In using the term "application" in this connection, Chladenius is borrowing a concept from legal and theological hermeneutics, that of *applicatio*, and investing it with a new meaning. This emendation is connected with his interest in establishing a general theory of interpretation. The essential features of this theory appear most clearly in the modifications to which Chladenius subjects the concepts and ideas derived from traditional hermeneutics. The phenomenon of application is closely connected to the interpretation of religious and legal texts insofar as these are meant, as doctrinal or legal opinions, to point beyond themselves and to function in a normative way. Such texts are interpreted not for their own sake or because one wishes to understand them, but with concrete cases, *casus*, in mind. This occurs most clearly in the pronouncement of judgments and the arguments offered to substantiate them; it is hardly less evident, however, in sermons, even if the cases cited there tend to be more general in nature. In the hermeneutics of Pietism, for instance in Rambach's *Institutiones hermeneuticae sacrae* (1723), the *subtilitas applicandi*, application, was added to the *subtilitas intelligendi*, understanding, and the *subtilitas explicandi*, interpretation[3] – quite possibly because of the increased influence of the preacher upon the souls of the faithful in Pietism. The element of application is, however, already present in the origins of theological hermeneutics, in allegoresis, the interpretation of the *sensus spiritualis*, which is important with respect to Chladenius. Typological interpretation can be understood as the application of the Old Testament to the story of the life and sufferings of Christ witnessed in the New Testament. The Scholastic discrimination of the four levels of meaning of the Scriptures is entirely based on the application of a passage. The allegorical meaning (which is identical with the typological) relates the passage to the story of the life and sufferings of Christ. In the interpretation of tropological or moral meaning, the passage is applied to the situation of the individual, as instructions about how to lead one's life. In the interpretation of anagogical meaning, finally, the frame of reference is eschatology. This is important to an understanding of Chladenius' hermeneutics because his distinction between the straightforward and mediated senses represents a generalized and secularized reformulation of the old distinction between the *sensus litteralis* and the *sensus spiritualis*, undertaken in the interest of establishing a *general* theory of interpretation. It is within the framework of this modification that we should view his reformulation of the concept of application, a concept which previously belonged to the *sensus spiritualis* and now becomes attached to the "mediated sense."

Chladenius makes application a necessary element of the mediated sense. It is not only religious and legal texts – characteristically classified as normative and distinguished from, among other things, literary and historial writings (as for instance in Emilio Betti's theory of interpretation) – which are always *applied*, but also – and no less so

---

[3] Developed in Gadamer's *Truth and Method*, p. 307.

– precisely literary and historical texts, according to Chladenius. What Chladenius means by this is clarified in the following sentences from §425:

The understanding which is imparted to the reader directly by the words of an historical passage[4] comprises only one part of the complete understanding of that passage. For by virtue of an inborn capacity, our soul immediately begins to employ the concept derived from those words and to think all manner of other things in connection therewith; which thoughts, once having been introduced, are incorporated into the understanding of the passage, since they were elicited and brought forth by the passage. The effects which our soul can produce because we have read and understood a particular book are called the *application* of the book.   (§425, pp. 308f.)

Thus, for Chladenius, the application is neither restricted to particular types of writing, nor is it – as in a sermon or legal commentary – a specific act which, though based on the reading of a passage, is not accomplished simply by reading the passage. Rather, application occurs for Chladenius whenever a text is read and understood – the application is the effect exerted by the text on the soul of the reader, it is the activity of the soul that is occasioned by the received text. To this extent Chladenius' theory of application as a necessary component of the meaning of a passage is stamped with the same orientation towards the psychology of reception that we find in Enlightenment aesthetics. Just as it was inconceivable for the authors of early- and mid-eighteenth-century poetics to ignore in their descriptions and definitions of a literary genre the effect which this genre was supposed to exert on the reader or spectator, so too was it necessary for Chladenius to postulate that, over and above the particular forms of legal and theological application exhibited in judgments and sermons, the effect of a text was universally relevant to its interpretation.

However, just as the goal of a general theory of interpretation goes hand in hand with the thesis of content-specificity, so here too we find that distinctions are made on the basis of the type of text to be interpreted. The previously cited definition of the application, or mediated sense, of a passage as "those concepts or ideas [...] which are brought forth and elicited by the straightforward sense gleaned from a passage" (§683, p. 528) is, significantly, only the result of an enumeration of the different forms of application classified according

---

[4] Chladenius speaks of "an historical passage" because he makes this point in a chapter on the "Auslegung der Historischen Bücher" ["Interpretation of Historical Works"], but what he says is not restricted to history.

to the type of book involved, whereby Chladenius mentions only historical and dogmatic books, since literary and legal texts were to have been treated in a later installment of his theory of interpretation. In §683 Chladenius writes:

In order to gain clearer insight into the nature of the applications, or mediated sense, of a passage, we must consider the various types of this sense, one by one [...]. That is to say, in the case of historical passages the application consists of the following: that one (1) learns of an historical event from it; (2) demonstrates an historical episode from it; (3) distinguishes general concepts from specific cases; (4) draws a moral from the event; (5) achieves vivid knowledge [*lebendige Erkäntniß*] of the event. In the case of didactic books, however, and the passages contained therein, the applications were: (1) that one attributes the doctrine to the author; (2) that one is persuaded by the doctrine presented in the passage; (3) that one appeals to it in other treatises; (4) that one draws logical conclusions from it; (5) that one receives vivid knowledge from it. (p. 528)

Each one of these points refers to a paragraph in which the specific form of application is illustrated by examples. Concerning the vivid knowledge which concludes the list of applications for both historical and dogmatic books, Chladenius writes:

Knowledge of the truth of a doctrine is called vivid knowledge insofar as it exerts an influence on our will and our actions. Not all knowledge which influences our will is called vivid knowledge. Many people have knowledge of the Christian religion and this knowledge motivates them to mock it; the Turks also have knowledge of it and are induced thereby to persecute it. No one would speak of vivid knowledge in either case, despite the fact that their knowledge does have an influence on their will. On the other hand, whoever honors, defends, and spreads the Christian religion for the sake of its truth does have vivid knowledge of it. (§474, pp. 341f.)

Chladenius goes on to distinguish the following degrees of vivid knowledge:

(1) Knowledge of a truth can cause an inclination or disinclination which, however, not being sufficiently strong or lasting, fails to erupt in overt action; (2) through knowledge of the truth, our spirit may be so moved that it erupts in overt actions, among which we would reckon the extreme passions, such as anxiety, extreme anger; (3) knowledge of the truth can transform our will in such a manner that it will respond in a similar way to certain situations which are similar: for example, those who have witnessed a conflagration generally treat light and fire with caution; (4) a truth can cause a transformation of our entire will, such that the consequences are expressed in all of our voluntary acts. Everyone knows of examples, for instance, in which

a sharp rebuke or a terrible accident has suddenly made people more withdrawn, pious, cautious, which response, furthermore, is expressed even in the most trivial of acts. The highest degree of vivid knowledge is to be found in the case of revealed truths, where these result in a conversion of the persons in question. (§486, pp. 353f.)

That Chaladenius considers "vivid knowledge" part of the "complete sense/understanding" of a passage can be understood only within the framework of the psychology of reception characteristic of his age. In this framework the passage is neither hypostasized nor viewed solely from the vantage of authorial intention; rather, all the concepts "which can be stimulated by the passage in question" (§674, p. 518) belong to its complete understanding.

The third component of the complete meaning of a passage which Chladenius isolates in addition to its straightforward and mediated senses is the "digression." This element shows us most clearly that, despite the theoretical perspective just outlined, the question of agreement between author and reader, the question of the identity between intended and understood meaning, is not an irrelevant criterion. It indicates to us moreover that the connection between the two hermeneutical principles – referring to intention and referring to effect – is really *the* central problem of Chladenius' theory of interpretation. In §690 he writes:

The mediated sense consists of those things which the soul continues to think of and feel after it has called to mind the things contained in the straightforward sense, and this occurs through the application of all kinds of capacities of the soul. [...] Now, because that which we call a digression is also brought forth, on the occasion of reading a passage, by a particular capacity of the soul, it is therefore no easy matter to distinguish the applications from the digressions. Nonetheless, the differences should become clear in the following way. As long as in our thoughts we must still have the passage in mind by which the thoughts were stimulated, we are still dealing with the application of the passage. When, however, we no longer need to think of the passage, then the concepts involved are to be called a *digression*, even if they were stimulated by the passage. (pp. 535f.)

Chladenius states by way of example:

Nothing [is] more common than explicating a passage in one book by reference to a passage in another; and this is a matter of application. But if in regard to the passage to be interpreted I appeal to the author and his life, or to the times in which he wrote the book – as well may happen in accordance with the rules of memory and the imagination – then we are dealing with a digression [...]. (§690, pp. 536f.)

The contradiction in Chladenius, which is that of a hermeneutics based on a psychology of reception, is fully revealed in the following paragraph where he denies that what he had designated as the third component of the complete meaning of a passage or book in fact plays a role in establishing the sense of the passage or book. The paragraph reads:

Since [...] the imagination and memory function differently in every person, presenting things to one person on this or that occasion which cannot occur to other people even though they are knowledgeable, it follows (1) that every reader is inclined to his own particular digressions whenever such are in order; (2) that the author of a text, because he is not all-knowing, cannot anticipate the digressions, especially when they concern things which had not yet occurred in his time, or did not yet exist, or had not yet been invented; (3) that therefore an author of a book cannot be in agreement with his readers in regard to digressions, for which reason (4) they also do not belong to the meaning of the book and the passage, since the author has not expressed himself on this subject. (§691, pp. 537f.)

Fifty pages later, on the other hand, he states once again that the "meaning of a book includes the straightforward sense, the applications, and the digressions" (§736, p. 582). This contradiction, which Chladenius allows to stand, raises the fundamental question of whether it is even tenable to analyze meaning into isolated components (such as straightforward sense, application, and digression) whose relationship to the author's intention varies, or whether such an analysis does not rather contradict the unity of the process of understanding. Here as elsewhere, the opposition between an empirical methodology based on observation and a normative one determined by postulates emerges – an opposition inherent in rationalism. Chladenius is clear about the fact that one

might raise the objection against the certainty of the straightforward sense [...] that very many, indeed, almost all, words have besides their common meaning also an accidental meaning, a figurative meaning, a narrower and a more comprehensive meaning; a natural consequence of which variation of meaning seems to be that the author may be thinking something else in using certain words than what a reader can perceive in them. (§742, pp. 587f.)

Not only is Chladenius aware of this possible objection, but it is one of the merits of his work to have pursued this issue of the multiple meaning of words, and especially that multiplicity of meaning arising from their use in metaphors. However, alongside this insight "that there really are ambiguous ways of speaking" stands the other, normative one "that even though one finds the above-mentioned types of meanings in all languages, nonetheless sentences and entire texts can be composed in such a way that a reader will of necessity think the same thoughts in reading them as the author had in composing them" (§742, p. 588). Chladenius similarly dilutes his insight into the connection between the specific intention of a book and its genre by introducing the normative perspective. For the circle according to which an interpretation ought to be oriented by the author's intention, while the intention is dependent upon the nature of the work, which in turn first reveals itself in interpretation − this circle is broken by the postulate that "one [...] may presume and hope that every skillful writer will have composed and thought in his book in accordance with the rules set down for the writing of such a book" (§705, p. 551).

In this context, finally, the set of problems should be mentioned which Chladenius touches upon when he says that "the author of a text [can] not anticipate the digressions, especially when they concern things which had not yet occurred in his time, or did not yet exist [...]." This is the problem of the historicity both of the work and of readers' understanding of it, the problem of the effect of historical distance on the work's impact.

Chladenius, III

Chladenius is true to the postulates of the psychology of reception when he defines "complete understanding" by saying "a speech or written text [is understood] completely when one thinks of all the things which the words can awaken in us" (§155, p. 86). That this psychology of reception is also a true child of the Enlightenment is shown by the qualification he builds into the definition: "in accordance with reason and the rules governing the soul." However, such a conception of the meaning of a passage or text is not easily reconciled with the claim so characteristic of rationalism that words "nevertheless have their certainty of meaning, even if they at first appear to be ambiguous when one considers the passage only superficially" (§750, p. 595). This claim in turn implies that "interpretations have their certainty" too (§751, p. 596). But certainty cannot emerge as long as "meaning" is construed as the totality of thoughts awakened in the reader. Such thoughts exhibit a multiplicity that is individually as well as historically determined. The logical contradiction arises from Chladenius' insight that passages can also mean things which did not "enter the mind" of the author (§156, p. 87), together with the claim that certainty derives from what the author intended. This contradiction between the claims of the psychology of reception and those of rationalism is reflected in Chladenius' division of "complete meaning" into: a straightforward sense, a mediated sense, i.e., an application, and finally digressions, which do not share equal status with one another. In qualification of the conclusion that each of these is a part of "complete meaning," Chladenius argues that only *those* aspects of meaning in which agreement with the author's intention can be assumed may be interpreted with certainty, which is to say the "straightforward sense" but not the "digressions," whose inclusion in the "complete meaning" he sometimes affirms and sometimes denies. The status of the "mediated sense," i.e., of the applications, is left equally fuzzy.

To be sure, Chladenius distinguishes between applications that are "necessary" and those that are not; but even in the case of the necessary ones he acknowledges that they may not agree with those the author intended, that it can happen, on the contrary, that an author "differs from [his readers], or actually even disagrees with them." What is expressed here is "the difference, that the passages may be sometimes more, sometimes less fruitful for the reader [i.e., capable of provoking thoughts in him] than they seem to have been for the author" (§694, pp. 539f.). This discrepancy cannot be resolved within Chladenius' system. Chladenius is, therefore, forced to appeal to postulates which do not follow from his analysis, the results of which are in part negated by those postulates. By way of example, in §694, directly following his claim that an author does not always estimate the fruitfulness of a passage correctly, Chladenius says:

Because, however, speeches and written texts are to be viewed as explanations and thus are produced so that one may know the author's opinion, it follows that the author, just as he is in agreement with his readers as regards the straightforward sense, ought also to be in agreement with them as regards the mediated sense. To achieve this, no one has been able to cite any other rules or methods to be followed both by all readers, when they approach a book without an interpreter, and by the interpreter himself, than the following: that one ought to respect the author's intention and not overstep it. (§694, p. 540)

Now, we must ask to what extent Chladenius' notion of speeches and written texts as explanations can be incorporated by contemporary hermeneutics. First, however, a few of his statements about the author's intentions must be cited, for they clarify the presuppositions which underlie this notion.

The intention of an author in a passage or book, or in general in any presentation whatsoever, is *the limitation of the idea he had of the thing or in regard to the passage*. For example, Virgil introduces Dido into his books. He regards her as a princess who fled Tyre following the death of her consort and founded the city of Carthage, all of which occurred in ancient times about which people in his own age no longer knew very much. This idea is limited, for he imagined neither the years nor even the century in which she actually lived, nor how old she was at the time of her flight or the construction of the city, nor what her religion was, in none of which he had any interest. The circumstances he imagined were enough by themselves for him to create a pleasing, though tragic, adventure with Aeneas, whose circumstances he likewise did not imagine in a very individualized way. His aim throughout the entire story is to delight readers, for he knew that his meaning-full [*sinnreich*] way of composing was bound to please most readers. – One can thus appeal to the author's intention in two types of cases and remind the reader that he should not lose sight of it: (1) when he thinks of something while reading a passage which the author was not thinking of: in which case he is *overstepping the intention*; (2) when he fails to think of something in reading a passage which the author did think of: in which case the reader *overlooks* or *does not realize* the author's *intention*. When one of these two things occurs, or both occur simultaneously, one generally says that the reader has *neglected* or *lost sight of* the author's *intention*. By not overstepping the intention, but also by not overlooking anything, one will understand the author completely. For example, there are some readers of Virgil who, going beyond the concept of Dido given in the work, have discovered from other sources what century she lived in.　　　　　　　　　　(§695, pp. 541f.; second emphases Szondi's)

Such readers have objected that Virgil offends against verisimilitude, since Dido lived 300 years after Aeneas. This example is particularly instructive because, over and above what Chladenius intended, it illuminates his concept of literature and simultaneously makes it clear why he can place literary texts on a par with (not equate them with) historical, dogmatic, and legal texts and subsume them under the same concept of explanation, i.e., of a declaration in which the opinion of the author is made known.

The example Chladenius chooses is a work of literature that draws upon traditional material. The critics of Virgil whom he faults are those who play their knowledge of the traditional material off against Virgil's treatment of it. What is important here is that Chladenius does not defend Virgil by appealing to poetic license, since he is interested not in defending Virgil, but in understanding him, in learning what his intention was. In appealing to chronology, Virgil's critics are making use of knowledge about the subject matter, historical data, that the poet bracketed out in shaping his material. This confrontation with a form of criticism which measures the work against the facts of history would have been impossible had Chladenius chosen as an example a work based entirely on the author's invention.

More significant here is that Chladenius' definition of intention itself presupposes that the subject of literature is external to literature. Chladenius' definition of the intention of an author as "the limitation of the idea he had of the thing" is based on the premise that "the thing" does not evolve *in* the literary work but has its own reality independently of the work. It is only thus that Chladenius can treat literature, like historical and legal texts, as "explanations" in the sense not of *explicatio* but of *declaratio* (p. 540); it is only thus that he can see, in the prescription that one ought to respect an author's intention, a solution to the problem of reconciling the multiplicity of meanings postulated by the psychology of reception with certainty of interpretation. If contemporary hermeneutics objects to having recourse to authorial intention on the grounds that the intention can be surmised only from documents which are extrinsic to the work, which therefore condemn the work to heteronomic status, this objection does not endanger Chladenius' theory, for his notion of literature is not absolutist. Literature, like philosophical or historical texts, is concerned with a subject matter about which it expresses the idea of the author. The reader may very well have different knowledge of the subject matter or other knowledge bearing on it. If, however, as Chladenius says, he wishes for the sake of certainty to be in agreement with the author with regard to both the straightforward and the mediated senses, then he must abstract from this other knowledge.

This means, however, that it would be senseless to oppose to Chladenius' chosen example – i.e., Virgil's presentation of Dido – examples which, because their subject matter does not exist outside of literature, would allow neither a criticism based on comparing literature with its model nor Chladenius' definition of intention as the author's limitation of the idea he has of a subject. What we must bear in mind is rather that *this* conception of literature underlies Chladenius' hermeneutics. What may appear to us as the exception – literature whose peculiarity is recognized through the contrast with its model – was for two reasons not the exception in Chladenius' time. First, from antiquity the connection with a model had been constitutive of the two most important genres, the epic and tragedy – in contrast, as is well known, with comedy. Second – and this is the decisive point – in the relationship of literature to a pre-existing historical-mythical subject matter as in epic and tragedy, the model recurs which dominated the entire conception of literature at that time, namely, that of the imitation of nature.[1] Thus lyric poetry too appeared to the eighteenth century as *imitatio naturae*, that is, of emotions belonging to human nature, with the result that a poem – in Chladenius' terminology – could be regarded as an explanation in which the author's view of a subject, his view, for example, of a specific emotion,

---

[1] On overcoming the principle of imitation, see Peter Szondi, "Antike und Moderne in der Ästhetik der Goethezeit," in Szondi, *Poetik und Geschichtsphilosophie I. Studienausgabe der Vorlesungen*, vol. 2 (Frankfurt am Main, 1974).

was expressed. The change that occurred during the transition from the eighteenth to the nineteenth century in the assumptions underlying poetics is illustrated especially dramatically by the history and theory of the novel, the genre which became the most characteristic of the nineteenth century.[2]

It is against this background that we should view one of Chladenius' theses which not only presents the key premise of his hermeneutics but also contains one of the points at which a contemporary hermeneutics will have to diverge from it. §680 also states:

All passages deal with some subject matter and contain either historical material or a universal principle. Since the straightforward sense is that which is presented to us by the words of a passage, we receive an idea and knowledge of a particular subject matter from every passage that we read and understand. For this reason the idea of a subject which constitutes the straightforward sense of a passage can be regarded in two different ways: (1) insofar as it is a concept and idea which is indicated, intended, and brought forth by words – or, in short, insofar as it is a meaning of the passage; (2) as knowledge about the subject matter which is treated in that passage.

(p. 525)

This duality of viewpoint – which, by the way, is without consequences in Chladenius' theory of interpretation – is possible only because both views are grounded in the same notion. With regard to the relevance of Chladenius' theories for a contemporary hermeneutics, however, the following consequences can be drawn. On the one hand, it has become clear that what makes it possible to view historical and dogmatic texts on a par with literary texts or, put another way, to unite specialized hermeneutics in a general hermeneutics, lies in the conception of literature as *imitatio naturae*. On the other hand, a break even more radical than the earlier one with imitation theory underlies our own concept of literature. For with the inception of absolute poetry in the late nineteenth century and of abstract poetry in the twentieth century not only did the connection of literature with a preexisting reality – that was once to be imitated – disappear, but a literature became possible that renounces the creation of an object through the medium of fiction, a literature that has instead become its own subject matter and that owes its unity to the diverse interrelations of word elements – by no means only

[2] Important contributions on these issues may be found in the volume *Nachahmung und Illusion,* ed. Hans Robert Jauß (Munich, 1964).

44

semantic elements – rather than to the coherence of the invented object or the fictional world.[3]

If contemporary hermeneutics is to take this historical transformation of the concept of literature into consideration as well as the transformation of literature itself, if it is not to forgo the possibility of dealing with the literary works of the last hundred years, then it must do more than revise Chladenius' thesis according to which all passages deal with a subject matter and understanding a passage is to be regarded as acquiring knowledge about the subject treated therein. Rather, what especially requires revision is Chladenius' notion of the meaning, the "sense," of a passage, since this conception assumes the preexistence of a subject matter. In light of the transformation of the concept of literature, moreover, unifying the various specialized hermeneutics in a general theory of interpretation becomes a dubious undertaking, for, as we see it, literature does not deal with an external subject matter or communicate insights in the same way that, say, historical or legal texts do. What was termed the postulate of content-specificity, which represents, as it were, a built-in corrective to this tendency toward generalization, also becomes problematic. When Chladenius postulates that the author's intention or the application, i.e., the mediated sense of a text, is always specific, that is, dependent on the nature of the material treated in the text, he is assuming that the subject matter with which, say, legal, historical, philosophical, and literary texts deal itself varies, while overlooking the possibility of differences in the way texts relate to their subject matter. The possibility that a literary work might not have preexisting subjects but that these subjects might be brought into being by the work, or might be identical with it, was necessarily inconceivable to a hermeneutics that remained within the framework of the *imitatio naturae* theory – no one would hold that against an author who lived in the mid-eighteenth century. We have seen that, from the standpoint of Chladenius' system, content-specificity and genre-specificity are synonymous. Hence, it is clear how this system must be revised: we must recognize that these concepts are not identical. The fact is that, because of its deep roots in the tradition of *imitatio naturae*, genre-specificity proves to be a more appropriate category than content-

---

[3] See Szondi's analysis of Mallarmé's "Hérodiade," in Szondi, *Das lyrische Drama des Fin de siècle. Studienausgabe der Vorlesungen*, vol. 4 (Frankfurt am Main, 1975), pp. 31–138; and Peter Szondi, *Celan-Studien* (Frankfurt am Main, 1972).

specificity. The various types of writing are distinguished from one another – historical from literary, but also within literature the individual genres – not only by the nature of their contents, but also by the different relation of each to its contents.

Just as we must revise Chladenius' notion of the meaning of a passage or text, so too must we reexamine his claim that a passage or text is correctly understood when agreement is achieved between author and reader, a claim I have repeatedly cited but so far not discussed in any depth. I will disregard the distinctions Chladenius makes, depending on whether the straightforward sense, the mediated sense, or the digressions are at issue. For what is important to this discussion is the connection between the theory of agreement and the historically conditioned premises of Chladenius' hermeneutics. Paragraph 677 states: "The straightforward sense is that about which the author of the passage and all his readers who understand the passage must be in agreement" (p. 522). Paragraph 681 refers to this and is supposed to show "to what extent the author is in agreement with his readers in regard to knowledge of and theories about the subject matter at hand" (p. 526). It says here:

Since the straightforward sense is at the same time knowledge of the subject matter which is treated in the passage, and the author of a passage is in agreement with all of his readers as regards the straightforward sense, it follows that: (1) if the author believes the proposition of his passage to be true and the reader also holds it to be true, then the author must agree with his readers as regards knowledge of the subject matter insofar as this knowledge is contained within the straightforward sense. (2) Further, since all truths are to be regarded as theories, the author must agree with all his readers as regards the theory of the subject matter treated in the passage insofar as the theories of the same subject matter are contained in the straightforward sense. (3) Since all passages are explanations, all readers therefore understand the explanation that the author has given about the subject matter treated in the passage, insofar as the explanation is contained in the straightforward sense. (pp. 526f.)

As so often with Chladenius, we wish to know whether the statements here apply to literature or only to historical and dogmatic (i.e., philosophical) texts, the only ones discussed at length in the completed part of his theory of interpretation (which, incidentally, as Lutz Geldsetzer has observed,[4] was written under the influence of Christian Wolff, whose book on logic contains a chapter on "Das Lesen

---

[4] See his introduction to Meier, *Versuch einer allgemeinen Auslegungskunst*, p. xi.

historischer und dogmatischer Bücher" ["The Reading of Historical
and Dogmatic Books"]). But not only does Chladenius maintain that
he has "explained and demonstrated the rules for interpreting general
truths as well as chronicles [*Historien*], whether they be presented
orally or in writing, and in such a manner that all the interpretations
of the remaining types of books can be reduced to this method" (§648,
p. 497). The example of Virgil's Dido has shown the extent to which
– and, above all, the concept of literature on the basis of which –
Chladenius can also define the intention of the author of a literary text
as "the limitation of the idea" which he "had of the subject matter"
(§695). Chladenius charges those critics with a false interpretation –
that is, one which oversteps Virgil's intention – who on the basis of
their own "chronological knowledge" (§696, p. 542) criticize the poet
for offending against the postulate of verisimilitude (because Dido
lived 300 years after Aeneas). And it is this example taken from
literature which leads him to the following theoretical paragraph:

Insight into a subject matter is knowledge of it insofar as we really imagine
what is contained in the subject matter. It stands in contrast to limitation, or
to the intention found in knowledge. Therefore (1) whoever has the same
knowledge as another about a subject matter must also have the same insight
as well as the same intention in regard to the subject matter. (2) Whoever has
more insight than the author of the passage oversteps the author's intention;
by contrast, whoever has less insight than the author does not realize his
intention. (3) Whoever has one and the same insight into a passage [subject
matter] as the author no longer needs to be reminded that he should respect
the author's intention. (§697, pp. 542f.)

The relevance of these theses to the example of Virgil is clear: the
critics mentioned by Chladenius overstep Virgil's intention on account
of their historical knowledge, whereas a person who knows neither
more nor less about Dido than Virgil presents has insight that
coincides with the author's intention so that he cannot deviate from it.
Between him and the poet there is agreement. But what sense are we
to make of this if the reader's insight into subject matter is itself
indebted to the work because the subject matter does not even exist
outside the work? The answer lies in the persistence of the concept of
imitatio naturae. As long as lyric poetry, say, is regarded as an imitation
of emotions, we can assume that we correctly understand or interpret
a sonnet on the death of the beloved, for example, whenever we have
the same insight into the subject matter, i.e., into the feelings of one
mourning the death of the beloved, as the poet – feelings, it is worth

noting, which, according to the view that prevailed at the time of Chladenius and was expressed in his theory of interpretation, neither the poet nor the reader actually had to feel. Agreement between author and reader is not established by means of empathy, by their feeling the identical emotions – which, after all, are not expressed but only imitated in the poem – it is established on the basis of their having the same insight into the nature of these emotions.

Concerning the problem of the agreement postulated by Chladenius, it should be noted further that a contemporary hermeneutics will have to reexamine this notion, not only with regard to literature, but also in relation to the interpretation of other kinds of writing as well. This problem has contemporary relevance in part because the phenomenon of agreement, of consent [*Einverständnis*] in the emphatic sense of the word, plays an important role in Gadamer's hermeneutics, a role, it seems to me, that urgently needs to be reexamined for its ideological presuppositions. We read, for instance, in *Truth and Method*:

Understanding means, primarily, to understand the content of what is said, and only secondarily to isolate and understand another's meaning as such. Hence the most basic of all hermeneutic preconditions remains one's own foreunderstanding, which comes from being concerned with the same subject. [...] Thus the meaning of "belonging" – i.e., the element of tradition in our historical-hermeneutical activity – is fulfilled in the commonality of fundamental, enabling prejudices.[5]

Gadamer seeks to overcome the aporias of historicism by appealing to a notion of effective-history [*Wirkungsgeschichte*] which rests on the same notion of tradition. "Temporal distance," he writes,

is not something that must be overcome. This was, rather, the naive assumption of historicism, namely that we must transpose ourselves into the spirit of the age, think with its ideas and its thoughts, not with our own, and thus advance toward historical objectivity. In fact the important thing is to recognise temporal distance as a positive and productive condition enabling understanding. It is not a yawning abyss, but is filled with the continuity of custom and tradition, in the light of which everything handed down presents itself to us.[6]

Gadamer rightly refers to Chladenius in just this context. For his theory of "point of view" cannot be separated from the fundamental feature of his hermeneutics which we have been discussing here, that

[5] Gadamer, *Truth and Method*, pp. 294–95.   [6] Ibid., p. 297.

is, the connection of the passage to a preexisting subject matter. For both Chladenius and Gadamer, this connection logically leads to postulating agreement or consent. The theory, which may be considered Chladenius' greatest contribution and a bold anticipation of the theory of the historical situatedness of cognition, has its limitations in the notion upon which it is based of the relationship between passage and subject matter, between understanding a passage and having an insight into the subject.[7]

The two chief orientations of hermeneutic practice, historical-grammatical and allegorical interpretation, developed because texts age, because of their historicity.[8] Chladenius reflected upon this fact in the introductory chapter of his book as well as in the theory of "point of view" he developed later. The concept of the unbelievable [*Unglaublichen*], a form of *obscuritas*, plays an important role in relation to historical writings. In §319 he writes:

A chronicle is told, or written, in order that the readers and listeners should believe it. If the story is in itself possible and if he who tells it is worthy of belief, then there exists no reason why we should not believe it. We see, however, that we do not want to believe a story when it seems to us unexpected, improbable, or fanciful. If it is nevertheless true, then our disbelief is a sign that we do not understand it; it follows that one does not understand true stories when the reason one disbelieves them is that they seem to be unexpected, improbable, or fanciful. Such stories therefore are in need of interpretation. (p. 196)

Chladenius sees in historical change one thing that can make a story unbelievable. Stories

can become unbelievable with the passage of time. For when the subject matter that the words point to changes imperceptibly, people will in time associate the chronicler's words with other thoughts, namely, with the idea of things that exists at that time, though they really ought to imagine those things in the manner of the time of the chronicler and of the event. But since we associate other concepts with the words, something may seem contradictory or incomprehensible to us that is perfectly natural and comprehensible in terms of the proper concepts [*eigentlichen Begriffen*]. For example, in Roman histories it is reported that many a Roman citizen had from ten to twelve thousand servants. Now, if this information were preserved but the true concept of a Roman citizen were to be forgotten with the passage of time, it would seem unbelievable to many that a citizen could have had so many more servants than today are found on the estates of counts, lords, or even princes. (§53, p. 22)

[7] See Chapter 5, pp. 57f.   [8] See Chapter 1, pp. 5ff.

The point of departure for Chladenius' reflections – corresponding to the centrality of subject matter in his hermeneutic conception – is the circumstance that "the subject matter that words point to changes imperceptibly." In his third chapter, which deals with "characteristics of words that should be considered in the interpretation of speeches and written texts" (p. 39), Chladenius returns to this matter, making the important observation that

when a thing changes gradually, [...] one can never find a sufficient reason to introduce a new word to replace an old one, and consequently the latter is always retained, even though the contemporary meaning is completely different from the original one. (§85, p. 43)

One consequence Chladenius mentions of such a change in meaning is that "a word that was previously employed only in serious speech may with time become ludicrous or derogatory" (§87, pp. 43f.).

The questionable nature of these observations derives from the assumed primacy of the object over the word, to which Chladenius' conception of the structure of meaning ascribes a merely signifying function. The problem appears already with the word "servant," an example he cites again in the context of his discussion of the gradual and imperceptible change undergone by things. Even if, as Chladenius says, the "severity of servitude is gradually mitigated by various laws" (§85, p. 42) and there has thus been a change in the situation, the sentence which states that "many a Roman citizen had ten to twelve thousand servants" will still seem unbelievable, but not because citizens or servants have changed with the passage of time. Rather, it will seem unbelievable because the words "citizen" and "servant" are used here instead of *civis* and *servus*, obscuring the fact that these words come from another language and therefore that they also represent a different historical reality. Thus the statement is un-believable not because the situation behind the façade of an unchanging word has changed, but because the German word is used to refer to something other than what it means. That Chladenius does not see this reflects the priority of objects over words that was characteristic of the thinking of his time. This is one of the central points upon which a contemporary hermeneutics must differ with his.

This necessity becomes still more evident when Chladenius discusses cases in which, as he sees it, meaning does not change. An "imperceptible change in the proper meaning of a word [...] does not take place when the things to which the words point always remain one and the same" (§88, p. 44). In marked contrast to his usual procedure, Chladenius gives no examples of this. Nor does he explain the examples he adduces in the two subsequent paragraphs in order to demonstrate the constancy of meaning in terms of objects that remain unchanged. Might not the absence of examples in the one case and the lack of explanation in the other indicate that Chladenius regarded the examples he gives of the constancy of meaning as examples of the constancy of the object as well? These are, on the one hand, concepts like "pain," but also "hard," "smooth," "green," "white," "red," and on the other hand concepts like "order," "necessity," "similarity." Where Chladenius designates the latter group "metaphysical words" (§90, p. 45), he speaks of the former only as words that present a "clear but very indistinct concept" (§89, p. 44). These are words that designate natural phenomena – sensations, as in the word "pain"; physical properties, as in the words "hard" and "white." It seems probable that Chladenius denied the possibility that these words shift meaning because they do not – as do the words "citizen" and "servant" – come from the realm of history, but from that of physics or metaphysics. He was probably not aware of his motivation here either, for while certain insights into the historicity of things and their signification through language were possible before the rise of historical consciousness, as Chladenius' theory of interpretation proves, the fundamental distinction between what is historical and what is not could not be made. Of course we cannot establish a contemporary literary hermeneutics merely by revising Chladenius' theories in the light of this distinction. We believe that the human idea of nature, if not nature itself, and hence also its linguistic expression, are historically determined and mutable. It follows, therefore, that even with a word like "white" we hesitate to rule out the possibility of a shift in meaning.

Chladenius did append the following comment to his contention that no imperceptible change in the proper meaning occurs when the things to which the words point remain immutable:

For even if it should happen that people began to use the word in a different, also proper [*eigentlich*] sense, this change of meaning would certainly soon be noticed by everyone, and would thus not occur imperceptibly, as happens in those cases where the things themselves change imperceptibly. (§88, p. 44)

Chladenius' allusion to "proper meaning" suggests that, in the case of the improper, the figurative, the metaphorical meaning, such a change is quite possible.[9] Here too, what makes Chladenius' thesis problematic is the mechanical distinction he draws between proper and improper meaning – as though the individual-historical element of the latter did not also affect what might originally have been the unhistorical component of the former. Even if the physical quality called white were not subject to historical change, in interpreting literary texts we would still take the historical element in the symbolic layer of the word and its field of associations into account – and not simply as the "improper meaning" alongside the "proper meaning" designating a physical datum. We do this because our contemporary understanding of literature simply does not recognize the pre-existence of the subject matter, in this case, a white object. Finally, it is worth noting that the history of language does not corroborate the constancy asserted by Chladenius either. For example, Chladenius claims that a word like "pain" "has always had the same meaning" and will "never change its meaning" (§89, p. 45), but the French word *travail* originally meant not "work" but "pain," "suffering."[10] That "suffering" remains "suffering" or, to recall our earlier example of *Boßheit* [malice, *archaic*: rage],[11] that "rage" remains "rage" down through the ages does not mean that language necessarily has to reproduce the immutablility of the object in semantic constancy. One reason it does not is that words obviously do not just signify things but also interpret them. As our conception of the relationship between word and thing, between language and reality, has changed, so has the foundation of hermeneutics as well as of poetics.

---

[9] See Chapter 5, pp. 58ff.
[10] *Robert* cites an example from Bossuet: "Les grands travaux que Notre Seigneur a soufferts." See also Littré, s.v. 2.   [11] See Chapter 2, pp 23ff.

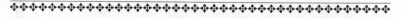

Chladenius, IV

It is not only in the context of semantic change, which he attributes to changes in the objects words denote, that Chladenius exhibits concern with the problem of historical change and its consequences for interpretation. His theory of "point of view" [*Sehe-Punckt*], of the perspectival bias in understanding, takes up the problem of historicality as well. Chladenius first expounds this theory in a chapter on the interpretation of historical books and takes it up again in a chapter on the interpretation of didactic books, i.e., philosophical works. Hence his theory of point of view is closely coupled with questions concerning historical writing and also, to a lesser extent, theoretical texts, but it appears that Chladenius had a general theory of interpretation in mind. In §308 he writes:

What happens in the world is viewed by different people in different ways, such that, if many people were to give a description of an event [*Geschichte*], we would encounter something particular to each one, even if each had perceived the thing correctly. These differences can be explained in part by the locations and positions of our bodies, which are different for each of us; in part by the different relationships we have to the things; and in part by our previous habits of thought, by virtue of which some of us are accustomed to paying attention to this, others to that. To be sure, it is commonly believed that for every object there is only one correct idea and, therefore, that if variations occur among narratives, one must be entirely right and the others entirely wrong. However, this rule accords neither with other common truths nor with a more precise knowledge of our soul.　　　　(p. 185)

Chladenius illustrates his claim that descriptions of an event vary with the position of the observer by reference to a battle with three observers, "of whom one is watching from a mountain on the side of the right flank of an army, the other from a hill on the side of the left flank, the third from behind the same army" (pp. 185f.), and who do not concur in their reports. The reasons are, first, that each of the observers notices different movements of the battle activity; second, that the same activity may look different when seen from a distance than it would when viewed close up. The situatedness of knowledge [*Standortgebundenheit der Erkenntnis*] with which Chladenius is concerned is, then, in the first instance to be understood as purely external, topographical. So the question arises as to whether this example is intended only as a metaphor for the relativity of knowledge – as "position" [*Standort*] is construed today in the sociology of knowledge. A second example used by Chladenius will help to answer this question. As with the battle, so it is, he writes, "with all occurrences; a rebellion will be viewed in one way by a loyal subject, in another by a rebel, in another by a foreigner, in another by a courtier, in another by a burgher or a peasant" (p. 187). Here, point of view refers not to physical position, but to social position or class and, by implication, the different interests each has in the outcome of the rebellion. Curiously, Chladenius passes over this implication: his theory of point of view has nothing to do with ideological criticism. Still, it is by no means merely concerned with differences arising from external, topographical considerations. On the contrary, his concept of point of view comprehends, to cite the definition in §309, "those conditions of our soul, body, and our entire person which make us, or are the reason we, perceive a thing in one way and not in another" (p. 187).

The term "point of view," says Chladenius, was

probably first used by Leibniz in a more general sense, since it occurred prior to this only in optics. One can best understand what he wished to signify therewith by reference to our definition, which clearly explains the same concept. We are using this concept here because it is indispensable if one is to account for the many and countless variations in the concepts people have of a thing. (p. 188)

Both the examples and the definition, especially the sentence just cited, make it clear that the concept of point of view refers not to the understanding of a text but primarily to the idea of a thing. One would thus expect to find it in epistemology, not in hermeneutics. However, since Chladenius believed that the interpretation of a passage or text was the same as knowledge of the subject matter treated in the passage or text, it is not possible to abstract from point of view in interpretation either. Here of course the question arises as to whose point of view is to be reflected in an interpretation. Just as words have different meanings today than when the author of a passage lived, and these differences make the passage obscure and in need of interpretation, so too will a passage need to be interpreted when the reader's point of view on the subject treated in the passage is different from the author's.

We judge the nature of the thing in accordance, namely, with the concept we have of it. Therefore, whatever is at odds with our concepts should, in our opinion, at the same time be at odds with the nature of the thing as well.
(§313, pp. 191f.).

For this reason, different people's reports concerning the same event may contradict one another "despite the fact that they have been conceived with such sincerity that each could swear to his own in good conscience." Then follows a crucial sentence: "Now to be sure, history can contain within itself nothing contradictory, but it can be presented to observers in such different ways that the reports about it do contain something contradictory" (p. 192). This sentence is crucial because it identifies the element which is capable of relativizing the contradictions that arise from the variety of points of view, namely, the thing itself, in the form of which history appears here. One of the next paragraphs states:

People commonly regard history and the idea of history as one and the same, and in many situations one may indeed regard them as the same. But where one is supposed to be concerned with the interpretation of history, one must indicate the distinction and make precise note of it. For it is not history as such but the idea of history which does not make sense to someone else that needs to be interpreted. (§318, p. 195)

The distinction between history and the idea of it is clear:

History is always one and the same, while the idea of it is varied and manifold; history contains nothing contradictory, whereas in the idea of history and in various ideas about it there may be something contradictory; in history everything has its sufficient cause, but in the idea of it things may occur which appear to happen without sufficient cause. (pp. 195f.)

Here we can see the epistemological premises of Chladenius' theory of the variety of points of view, but especially of his notion of how the consequences of this variety can be removed by interpretation.

Since Chladenius' work appeared in the year 1742, it is not surprising that his theory of knowledge is precritical – although it belongs to the Enlightenment. That is, what is to be known is no longer equated with the idea of it prescribed by those in power, such that any deviation is considered heresy, a sin not only against authority but – because of the equation of authority's view of things with reality – against reality itself. The role of one's own point of view in cognition is recognized and defended, i.e., the distinction between the thing in itself and our idea of it. This relativization is, however, uncritical, in the Kantian sense, because the question concerning the conditions under which cognition is possible is not raised. Despite his insight into the role of point of view, Chladenius did not question the knowability of things as they are in themselves. The insight that point of view conditions our knowledge of a thing in no way implies for him that the thing itself, as it truly is, cannot be known. To be sure, his hermeneutics does not logically require recourse to the thing itself in order to maintain certainty of interpretation in the face of the implications of point of view. For the variety that results from various points of view does not after all appear in the interpretations of a passage, and the passage, the object of interpretation, is not the thing – if this were the case, we would have the relativity of knowledge of contemporary hermeneutics. The thing is rather what is dealt with in the passage: history in historical texts, a truth in dogmatic writings. What varies are the ideas that author and reader have of this thing.

The variety of points of view will be a problem for interpretation to the extent that a passage can become unintelligible because the reader has a different idea of the thing that is the subject of the passage from the author. But this points the way for interpretation: the interpreter, Chladenius writes, "must imagine the history he wants to interpret from both points of view, partly as it appears to whoever finds it unbelievable, partly as the writer imagined it" (§324, p. 201). And clearer still in the final chapter of the *Einleitung*, in which, despite his insight into the manifold meanings of a passage, Chladenius makes the intention of the author of a text the guideline for the interpretation of the "straightforward sense" and the "necessary applications":[1] "In the historical interpretation of an author the interpreter ought to take note of the point of view from which he imagined the history and make this known to his pupil" (§707, p. 555). This means, however, that the aim of historical interpretation – the elimination of the historical distance between text and reader – is preserved even in the theory of point of view, the logical consequence of which ought to have been a recognition that it is not possible to separate oneself from one's own position and undo historical change. Just as historical-

---

[1] See Chapter 4, pp. 40ff.

grammatical interpretation holds onto the intended meaning and replaces the outdated sign, so too does the theory of point of view merge with the hermeneutic prescription to replace the reader's point of view with that of the author so as to hold onto the latter's idea of the thing.

Later, in the *Allgemeine Geschichtswissenschaft*, Chladenius worked out this theory and its applicability to historical hermeneutics in greater detail. There he attempts a typology of points of view in which he distinguishes: the interested party, the outsider, the novice, the friend and the foe, the higher and lower standpoint, the scholar, the happy person and the sad one, the barbarian. Compared with the example of rebellion cited in the *Einleitung*, this represents a step toward ideological criticism. However, Chladenius does not give up the postulate that one can transcend the refraction of the event through the different points of view and grasp history itself, in its objectivity. The methodology presented in the *Allgemeine Geschichts-wissenschaft* also conforms to this postulate. With historical works, Chladenius writes, a twofold procedure or method of interpretation is called for: (1) understanding the original document, i.e., the first telling, which is the basis of all further knowledge. This phase is supposed to proceed according to the rules of hermeneutics, to have recourse, therefore, to the author's intention and aim at agreement; (2) reflection upon and contemplation of the received document. In this phase the points made in the theory of point of view come into play. In other words, Chladenius' historical hermeneutics distinguishes between an interpretation of the original document, which leaps over historical distance and abstracts from one's own position, and reflection upon the historical distance and one's own point of view.

If we wished to transfer this double procedure to literary hermeneutics, we would end up with a distinction between historical-grammatical interpretation and interpretation based on effective-history. In making this transfer we should not of course forget that the application Chladenius himself would have made to literary texts would have been conditioned by a conception of the text according to which literature, no less than historiography, refers to a preexisting subject matter. For this reason the theory of "point of view" relates not to the historicity of the understanding of texts but to the changing ideas about the subject matter treated in the texts.

A critical examination of Chladenius' theories of interpretation and of point of view in terms of contemporary hermeneutics will raise the objection to his precritical epistemology that one cannot have both the thing in itself and the theory of the subjectivity of knowledge (which would have to be purchased at the cost of the thing in itself). If we wish to take the opposite position that objectivity of knowledge can be attained only by taking into account its subjectivity, not by dipping into a separate reservoir of "straightforward" understanding, then we must recognize that Chladenius' theory of point of view may be regarded only in a very limited sense as a precursor of later theories of the historical situatedness of knowledge, at least with regard to literary texts. And one of the reasons for this lies in the concept of *imitatio naturae*, which held unbroken sway in Chladenius' time. The overthrow of this concept in the late eighteenth century brought, as it were, a new point of view to power, which continues to condition our understanding of literature today. It is thus impossible to bracket out the more recent view according to which literature creates its own object while reading the literature written under the concept of *imitatio naturae* – and that is still the greater part of world literature. This impossibility suggests a need to make Chladenius' theory of the point of view much more radical.

In conclusion let us turn to the theory of metaphor outlined in Chladenius' theory of interpretation. Here, in his treatment of the interpretation of historical and dogmatic texts, Chladenius came closest to answering questions pertaining to literature. However, owing to the limitations resulting from the primacy of subject matter over expression in Chladenius' and his epoch's concept of literature, his answers are not entirely satisfactory for our purposes. A theory of metaphorical expression seems, more than other areas of poetics, to demand a language-oriented rather than a subject-matter-oriented concept of the text. But appearance here is deceptive. Chladenius devoted long discussions to metaphorical expression, figurative speech, in his chapters on the interpretation of historical and dogmatic texts instead of saving them for the planned continuation that was to treat literature. And these indicate that orienting interpretation toward the subject matter provided surprising possibilities for developing a theory of metaphor. The reason for this should become clear in our presentation of Chladenius' theory of metaphor.

Chladenius discerns the source of "figurative meaning" in the following situation: when one perceives a particular quality of a thing, another quality can be attributed to it which includes the former quality as a part.

For example, we see that a person is running and, as a consequence, gets from one place to another very quickly. By flying, birds likewise progress quickly from one place to another. For this reason the concept of fast movement is part of the concept of flying. Thus when we are presented with a fast movement, then according to the rule of the imagination, flying can occur to us; and thus it happens that we say of a person who is running or riding fast that he is flying. (§91, p. 46)

The definition of figurative, or metaphorical, meaning follows from this:

When we attribute a quality to a thing which, however, is only partially applicable to it, we will, when expressing our thoughts, also attribute to the thing a word which is not properly [*eigentlich*], but only in a certain sense, applicable to it. The word thereby attains a new meaning in that it points not to all but only to part of what it commonly means. For it is self-evident that whenever the thought which is associated with a word changes, a new meaning also arises. The meaning of a word where it does not mean all that it otherwise means is the *figurative sense* or the *figurative meaning* of the word. And it is this which contrasts with the proper meaning. (§92, pp. 46f.)

As primitive as it seems, this single example together with Chladenius' construal of it point up the critical differences between his own and the traditional theory of metaphor.

One difference is that Chladenius does not proceed from the unmetaphorical or literal expression, the *verbum proprium*, but from the thing to be designated. It is not that the word "running" is replaced by the word "flying"; rather, in imagining a person who is running, the quality of flying is attributed to him in place of that of running. This attribution of an alien quality, which is the origin of metaphorical language for Chladenius, points up a second difference between his theory and the theory of metaphor propounded by ancient rhetoric: Chladenius does not conceive of metaphor as an abbreviated simile. To say that a person flies does not in Chladenius' view presuppose a comparison between man and bird; even less does it presuppose that magical equation of man and bird of which the explanation of metaphor has been viewed as an after-the-fact rational interpretation.[2] Rather, when the quality of flying is attributed to a person – although he is flying only insofar as the fast movement which defines running is an element of flying – flying means something other than it does when said of a bird. This is the reason Chladenius does not distinguish

---

[2] On the traditional theory of metaphor, see Heinrich Lausberg, *Handbuch der literarischen Rhetorik*, 2 vols. (Munich, 1960), pp. 285–91, §558ff.

between the proper and figurative – or improper – *expression*, nor between the *verbum proprium* "running" and the metaphor "flying," but between the "figurative" and the "proper" meaning of the same word, "flying." It is necessary to inquire into the significance of these differences for the theory of metaphor as well as into the suppositions which underlie them.

In making not the *verbum proprium* but the thing the point of reference in his explanation of metaphor, Chladenius is following the premise of his entire hermeneutic theory according to which a passage represents the author's explanation of some subject matter and communicates his view of it. This notion may be disadvantageous to the understanding of literature because it refers literature to something supposed to preexist it, whereas this something, the subject matter, may equally well first be created by literature; but it does have the advantage with respect to the theory of metaphor that the metaphorical expression is not relativized by reference to the *verbum proprium*. This is advantageous because the *verbum proprium* of metaphorical expression is much less present, much less immanent in literature than the subject matter. According to our contemporary understanding, the latter does not preexist literature, though it may well preexist the metaphor, if not as an aspect of empirical reality, then as a component of the content of the metaphor, as which it became part of the metaphor. But the concept *verbum proprium* denotes a word which the literary work specifically did *not* use in the metaphorical passage. That a metaphorical expression has recourse to the subject matter and to the meaning that the same expression has as a non-metaphorical expression shows metaphorical language on the one hand as a way of experiencing reality and on the other as a modification of the preexisting language. By contrast, talk of the *verbum proprium* degrades metaphor to a simple question of expression, of designation, to a question that has no effect either on our conception of things or on the meaning of words. Thus, linking literature to a pregiven world of facts both elevates the dignity of the metaphorical expression since, owing to its connection with things, it is regarded as a mode of cognition; and leads, paradoxically, to an increase in the significance that accrues to language itself and to reflection on language.

It is against the background of these insights that the following questions should be viewed: that of the justification of "figurative" expression, that of the role of metaphorical language in historical and philosophical texts, that of the relationship between metaphor and the formation of concepts, and finally that of the interpretation of metaphorical passages. Concerning the question of the reasons for metaphorical expression, Chladenius writes in §122:

Two reasons are commonly given for the use of metaphorical words: that one uses such words in part out of necessity, but also in part to express a thing in a pleasing way. The necessity that impels us to use a word in the figurative sense consists of nothing other than the desire to express ourselves as completely as possible and, therefore, to employ the most emphatic word. Hence, when we use a metaphor out of necessity and the chosen word really serves to express the subject in detail, such a metaphor is right. The other reason we use metaphorical words is, upon closer examination, not distinct from the first. For if one wishes to present a subject with grace and in a manner that is not common, one must, as it were, turn the subject over and exhibit its special qualities. But since these qualities normally do not have their own words and names, one must either make use of general words or present the subject in detail [i.e., giving all its particulars, thus, precisely] through metaphor and in one single concept. (pp. 67f.)

And after he has analyzed, by way of example, the Latin phrase *sulcare mare*, to plow a furrow, for the movement of a ship, Chladenius continues:

Thus in this case too the poets have used metaphor out of necessity, for they did not know any way to express their concept more emphatically than through this expression. Therefore, to use a metaphor for the sake of greater grace is but a special case of metaphor used out of *necessity* [...]. (p. 68)

With this assertion Chladenius revises in an exceedingly fruitful way views inherited from ancient rhetoric that were still considered valid in his day. Thus in Gottsched's *Critische Dichtkunst* [*Critical Poetics*] (1730), the fourth edition of which appeared a decade after Chladenius' *Einleitung*, we read:

In the third book on the orator, Chapter 38, Cicero explicitly teaches that the improper meanings of words first arose, to be sure, due to the defects and insufficiency of languages, but that thereafter they were also used for grace and ornamentation: just as in the beginning we invented and introduced clothing to cover our nakedness, but subsequently wore it for reasons of splendor.[3]

The concept of a defect in language which forces us to use metaphorical expressions is thus known to ancient rhetoric: a lexical

---

[3] Johann Christian Gottsched, *Versuch einer Critischen Dichtkunst*, 4th rev. edn. (Leipzig, 1751; rpt. Darmstadt, 1962), p. 259.

defect, the lack of a *verbum proprium*, is according to Quintilian the condition for the "necessary" metaphor.[4] Gottsched's definition of metaphor shows, however, how insignificant a role this genesis and therewith the element of necessity in metaphorical expressions play in Enlightenment poetics:

The metaphor is a figurative turn of phrase in which one replaces a word which fits the thing in its proper sense with another which has a certain similarity to it and thus involves a brief simile.[5]

Here the presence of the *verbum proprium*, which is used to deny the necessity of metaphor, has become part of the definition of metaphor, whereas its necessity was one of the reasons Quintilian had cited to justify the evil of displacing a *verbum proprium* from its context.[6]

By way of contrast, concerning the metaphors which he quotes from an ode by Fleming, "the adamantine waters, the amorous stars," Gottsched observes: "in the proper sense one would have had to say: the clear waters, the twinkling stars," but the poet leads us to completely different concepts by his ingenious words; the words nearest to hand were not good enough (i.e., were too simple) for him: "he fetches from afar quite uncommon thoughts, which yet fit the subject matter and make images very pleasing to the mind when it recognizes the similarities between them."[7] Chladenius would have explained these examples in a very different way. Instead of asserting, on the one hand, that the poet ought to have said "the clear waters" in place of "the adamantine waters," his point of departure would have been the insight that the expression "the clear waters" did not completely communicate the poet's idea of the subject, that he did not find in the language a more precise word for the quality of water he perceived. On the other hand, he would not have been satisfied with the assertion that the metaphorical use of "adamantine" "makes images very pleasing to the mind," but would instead have observed in the use of the word in the improper sense the emergence of a new general concept.

Whenever we use a word in the figurative sense, a new, general concept arises in our mind. For when the word is used in the figurative sense it means only

---

[4] Quintilian, *Institutio oratoria*, Bk. 8, Chap. 6, Paragraph 34, tr. H. E. Butler (Cambridge, Mass., 1921), vol. 3, p. 321.

[5] Gottsched, *Versuch einer Critischen Dichtkunst*, p. 264.

[6] Quintilian, *Institutio oratoria*, vol. 3, p. 321.

[7] Gottsched, *Versuch einer Critischen Dichtkunst*, p. 264.

a part of what it otherwise means. But the word is applied to another subject, and thus a part of its proper meaning is joined to the other particulars of the other thing. The portion of the common meaning that is retained in the figurative use can, accordingly, be separated out (abstracted) and regarded as a general concept or genus, such that the proper and the figurative sense constitute two *types* (species) of the same thing. (§94, p. 48)

In this way metaphor proves to be not external to thought but one of its specific possibilities or media.

If we keep in mind the two principal theses of Chladenius' theory of metaphor, that (1) the metaphorical expression always stems from the lack of a *verbum proprium* and (2) a new concept always results from the metaphorical use of a word, then we have an answer to the question of why figurative language, meaning-full [*sinnreich*] speech, is also at home in historical and dogmatic (i.e., philosophical) texts.

Chladenius calls the metaphor correct when it "is used for the sake of emphasis," i.e., when the metaphorical word expresses the subject with more precision than the *verbum proprium,*

such that if one did not wish to employ the metaphorical word, certain particulars either would not be indicated at all or would have to be noted with many words and through a paraphrase, which, however, could not occur without somewhat altering the concept itself. (§121, p. 66)

The implication is that metaphorical expression may be required by the subject matter itself, for the sake of its most precise possible characterization. By lifting it out of the aesthetic sphere and assigning it this function, which in ancient rhetoric was only one among others, Chladenius justifies its use in nonliterary descriptions, as for instance in historiography.

The significance of metaphor in philosophy derives, on the other hand, from its role in the formation of concepts.

Because general concepts are hidden within figurative uses of language, a sage can learn something from them, and figurative discourse is of use for more than just entertaining our imagination. Namely, one can derive general concepts from it which, when they are clearly explained, help extend the sciences. One will also find that nowadays one encounters lengthy treatises on some philosophical concepts which until recently were regarded as mere figurative discourse. Formerly it was only in poetic speech that man was called a little *world*, and one still says of a populous city: it is a world full of people. At present the concept of world is treated in philosophy in such a way that a large city, and even every individual, can be called a world in the proper, but also the philosophical, sense. (§96, p. 49f.)

This usage is only possible, according to Chladenius, because "to the common [...] and the figurative meaning of the word yet a third" (§99, p. 52) is added. The figurative use of a word allows a general concept to emerge in which the proper, or literal, and metaphorical meanings coincide. This general concept can be separated out. Even if it is referred to with the "common" word, one nevertheless has the word — for instance the word "world" — in a new meaning, namely, in that of the general concept. This is amplified by the word "scream":

> Everyone knows what *screaming* means. But an orator may perhaps say of a stone splattered with human blood: the stone is screaming. Through this figurative use of the word we obtain a general concept of screaming: namely, that it is the same as expressing something so clearly and obviously that everyone must of necessity pay attention to it. (§94, p. 48)

Chladenius goes on to say that because general concepts belong to the domain of reason, reason is required in the figurative use of words; that at the same time, however, imagination too plays a role. However primitive the examples may be, we should not underestimate the significance of this assimilation of metaphor to philosophy, a classification that couples reason and imagination. In contrast with the traditional view, dominant in philosophy even *after* Chladenius, that metaphors accomplish nothing for thought, Chladenius sketched out a different view, which, as I see it, was not worked out in detail until our time, in Hans Blumenberg's *Paradigmen zu einer Metaphorologie* [*Paradigms of a Theory of Metaphor*].[8]

To answer the question of how to interpret metaphorical words, Chladenius takes their two related functions in historical and dogmatic texts as a point of departure. In historical texts their function is emphasis, that is, the extra meaning that distinguishes the metaphorical expression from the *verbum proprium*. Emphasis is what legitimates metaphorical expression in the first place. In dogmatic texts their function is the general concept that the metaphorical use of a word elicits. This distinction also shows the content-specificity of Chladenius' theory of interpretation. This theory is designed as a general theory, which means that metaphor is not restricted to literature but conceived rather as a basic possibility for expressing subject matter. Nevertheless, as Chladenius sees it, the metaphorical use of a word differs depending on whether it occurs in an historical, a dogmatic, or — though he did not develop this idea — a literary text.

[8] Hans Blumenberg, *Paradigmen zu einer Metaphorologie* (Bonn, 1960).

Chapter 5

In philosophical texts, interpretation has the task of specifying the general concept contained in the metaphor. Chladenius claims that obscurity can arise here from the fact that although a separate concept may well have been joined with a metaphorical one, it still might not be

the same one that the author had in mind. For since a word can have more than one metaphorical meaning, it depends on the remainder of the reader's ideas whether he connects this or that general concept with it. Whoever does not possess just the same knowledge as the author of a didactic text, therefore, will not think as he in response to the metaphorical words.

(§565, pp. 428f.)

Thus, for example, a person unacquainted with Leibniz's philosophy could think that he was pointing to the element of determinism in his comparison of the soul to a machine. Such a reader regards the determinism expressed in the machine's movements as a characteristic trait which he then takes to be the general concept of the passage. For Leibniz, however, it is rather the circumstance that both the soul and the machine contain the source of their movements within themselves which constitutes their beauty, while he considers determinism among their limitations and imperfections. Thus, with philosophical texts metaphor must be interpreted by reference to the author's system. Here too the mode of interpretation proves to be dependent upon the genre of the text, for such a frame of reference presupposes the logical consistency of a book – something which is certainly in keeping with the definition of philosophy but not of literature.

It is possible here only to refer in passing to the question of whether the concept of philosophy is also subject to historical change, such that, for instance, a contemporary philosophical text would, like literature, have its own temporality. This would mean that knowledge could be falsified in the course of intellectual progress without necessarily being false within the passage in which it is found. I must likewise pass over the question of whether reference to the system which is first constituted by the totality of passages leads to the hermeneutic circle and to what extent this circle differs from the one which emerges in an analogous way with a literary text.

In historical texts interpretation must determine not the general concept but the "emphasis." Emphasis is a quality of a word that expresses something "in more detail," i.e., more precisely than other words which "indicate the same thing only to a certain extent" (§114, p. 62). Determining emphasis, which Chladenius by no means restricts to the interpretation of metaphor, is one of the main tasks of hermeneutics. It is based on the important insight that "one does not readily encounter two equivalent words in a language" (§111, p. 60). But how can the emphasis of a word be determined?

One must turn for help to other reports which treat those particulars in which the historian is interested. Those passages which deal with the same event are parallel passages, and consequently we see how we can discover the emphasis of metaphorical words from a comparison of the parallel passages.

(§393, p. 278)

The significance of Chladenius' theory of interpretation lies not least of all in its material character,[9] as his discussion of the parallel passage method, among other things, confirms. We can consider the potential misuses of this method and the rules by which Chladenius hopes to preclude such misuses in the context of discussing another general hermeneutic theory, that of Georg Friedrich Meier.

[9] See above, p. 16.

6

Meier, I

It is one of the aims of a critical examination like the one we are pursuing here, in lieu of a purely historical presentation or a new hermeneutics, to reveal the historical determinateness of hermeneutic theories. The traditional notions of Enlightenment hermeneutics, to which the philological and theological contemporaries of Weimar Classicism and German Idealism formulated a counterposition, appear in another hermeneutic theory from the mid-century which differs from Chladenius' work on important points despite their common descent from the philosophy of Leibniz and Wolff. This is *Versuch einer allgemeinen Auslegungskunst* [*Toward a General Theory of Interpretation*] (1757) by Georg Friedrich Meier, who lived from 1718 to 1777 and was professor of philosophy in Halle. A disciple of Wolff's disciple Alexander Gottlieb Baumgarten, the author of the *Aesthetica*,[1] Meier published *Anfangsgründe aller schönen Künste und Wissenschaften* [*Basic Premises of All the Fine Arts and Sciences*] in 1748, which earned him the name of co-founder of German aesthetics.[2] Among his works a *Metaphysik* (1755–59) and a *Vernunftlehre* [*Theory of Reason*] (1752) ought also to be mentioned. At the time, all of these works were more highly regarded than the *Versuch einer allgemeinen Auslegungskunst*; and even histories of hermeneutics, owing undoubtedly to their theological or philosophical bias, have not paid it the attention it deserves. Not until Lutz Geldsetzer arranged for a new printing in 1965[3] did Meier's *Auslegungskunst* again become accessible and reenter discussion.

If one is coming from Chladenius, the first thing about this work to catch one's eye is a superficial difference. In contrast to Chladenius'

---

[1] Alexander Gottlieb Baumgarten, *Aesthetica*, 2 vols. (Frankfurt am Oder, 1750–58).

[2] See Ernst Bergmann, *Die Begründung der deutschen Ästhetik durch Alexander Gottlieb Baumgarten und Georg Friedrich Meier. Mit einem Anhang: G. F. Meiers ungedruckte Briefe* (Leipzig, 1911).   [3] See p. 18, n. 7, above.

comprehensive work, which treats the subject in all its detail and with numerous examples, Meier's *Auslegungskunst* is a sketch, more the scaffolding for a hermeneutics than a hermeneutic theory. The work served as a compendium, a manual for Meier's lectures in his professorial capacity. Even in Hegel's time lectures were still based on one's own or someone else's compendium. The purpose of lectures was not to transmit knowledge – that function was and is performed incomparably better by books. Rather, they were designed for the elucidation and discussion of a text that lay before everyone in the audience. Although it was certainly possible to criticize someone else's compendium, the compendium was assumed to have a certain validity and to reflect a consensus in the discipline. Nineteenth-century individualism emancipated the lecture from the compendium, without, of course, being able to guarantee the originality of what was presented in lecture. As criticism of the traditional lecture grows ever louder today, it may be useful to call to mind this historical development, and possibly replace the traditional "large lecture" with a research group format or a colloquium in which an assigned text would be illuminated and discussed not monologically but in a group.[a]

What distinguishes the *Auslegungskunst* in a less superficial way from Chladenius' hermeneutics is the basis for its claim to being a general theory. Chladenius too aimed at a general theory of interpretation. But the explanatory character of the passage seemed to him to be the common denominator among the specialized branches of hermeneutics: every passage, and thus every text, represents a declaration, the author's explanation of a subject. Chladenius' hermeneutics is thus a hermeneutics of the text. By contrast, Meier defines the art of interpretation as "the science of the rules which enable the meaning of signs to be recognized" (§1, p. 1). His hermeneutics is a hermeneutics of signs and thus ought to be viewed in the context of the general theory of signs, or semiology, developed by Saussure and represented today by, for example, Roland Barthes. Owing to its conception of the sign, however, Meier's hermeneutics remains firmly anchored in the optimistic Enlightenment philosophy

---

[a] Szondi is alluding to the pressure for university reform that constituted one of the goals of the radical student organization and action which swept West Germany in the 1960s. It was especially strong at the Free University in Berlin where he taught.

of Leibniz and Wolff, and thus, as we shall see, even in its most formal aspect has an historically specific intellectual content.

When Meier subsumes the art of interpretation under the theory of "characteristic," or science of signs, and says that it "derives its principles from the general theory of characteristic" (§3, p. 2), he is evidently referring to the general theory of characteristic worked out by the twenty-year-old Leibniz in his dissertation *De arte combinatoria* (Leipzig, 1666), although the concept of the sign had already been fundamental to the interpretive theory of patristic hermeneutics. Augustine's *De doctrina christiana*, written around the year 400 and highly influential for the biblical hermeneutics of later times, proceeds from a definition of subject matter and sign. In the second chapter of the first book he writes:

All doctrine concerns either things or signs, but things are learned by signs. Strictly speaking, I have here called a "thing" that which is not used to signify something else, like wood, stone, cattle, and so on; but not that wood concerning which we read that Moses cast it into bitter waters that their bitterness might be dispelled [Exod. 15.25], nor that stone which Jacob placed at his head [Gen. 28.11], nor that beast which Abraham sacrificed in place of his son [Gen. 22.13]. For these are things in such a way that they are also signs of other things. There are other signs whose whole use is in signifying, like words. For no one uses words except for the purpose of signifying something. From this may be understood what we call "signs"; they are things used to signify something. Thus every sign is also a thing, for that which is not a thing is nothing at all; but not every thing is also a sign. And thus in this distinction between things and signs, when we speak of things, we shall so speak that, although some of them may be used to signify something else, this fact shall not disturb the arrangement we have made to speak of things as such first and of signs later. We should bear in mind that now we are to consider what things are, not what they signify beyond themselves.[4]

Then, at the beginning of the second book, Augustine turns to signs and thus also to things as signs.

A sign is a thing which causes us to think of something beyond the impression the thing itself makes upon the senses. Thus, if we see a track, we think of the animal that made the track; if we see smoke, we know that there is a fire which causes it.

---

[4] Augustine, *On Christian Doctrine*, tr. and intro. D. W. Robertson, Jr. (Indianapolis, 1958), pp. 8–9.

There then follows the distinction that would remain the basis for the classification of hermeneutics in Meier's work:

Among signs, some are natural and others are conventional. Those are natural which, without any desire or intention of signifying, make us aware of something beyond themselves, like smoke which signifies fire. It does this without any will to signify, for even when smoke appears alone, observation and memory of experience with things bring a recognition of an underlying fire. [...] Conventional signs are those which living creatures show to one another for the purpose of conveying, in so far as they are able, the motion of their spirits or something which they have sensed or understood.

Even biblical hermeneutics is concerned with such signs, Augustine writes, for "the signs given by God and contained in the Holy Scriptures [...] were presented to us by the men who wrote them [down]."[5]

The reference to Augustine may help to clarify *e contrario* the specific presuppositions underlying Meier's use of the paired terms "natural and artificial" (Augustine says "conventional") signs – presuppositions that are overlooked if, like the editor of the Meier reprint, one is content to observe that this is the conventional distinction made by German Scholasticism.[6] It is not our aim here to trace the history of the theory of signs, but we do need to pinpoint and understand the difference between Augustine's conception of the natural sign and that of the philosophers of the eighteenth century. In Augustine's example of a natural sign, the referential function is not essential to the smoke. It is observation and experience, he says, that allow us to perceive smoke as a sign by grounding our knowledge that fire is nearby when we can see only smoke. Meier's view stands in contrast to this. In §35, which introduces the section on the interpretation of natural signs, he states:

In this world, because it is the best, there exists the very greatest degree of general, signifying connection which is possible in a world. Consequently every single real part of this world can be a direct or indirect, a distant or close natural sign for any other real part of the world.   (p. 18)

What Meier means by "signifying connection" is the connection between sign and meaning. The meaning of a sign is the thing signified by it. Meier also understands the meaning as the intent of the

---

[5] Ibid., pp. 34–35.
[6] Geldsetzer, "Introduction," in Meier, *Versuch einer allgemeinen Auslegungskunst*, p. xviii.

sign. Whereas Augustine expressly states that the smoke does not "intentionally" refer to the fire which causes it, and thus that the signifying character of things is, as it were, external and incidental to them insofar as they are natural signs, the disciple of Leibniz and Wolff considers things, as components of the world, to be signs because the signifying connection constitutes the world. The signifying connection here is — wholly in keeping with Augustine's example of smoke — primarily a causal connection. §68 reads:

Since one can reason from the reality of the cause to the reality of the thing caused, and likewise, from the existence of the thing caused to the existence of the real cause, it follows that every cause that is a part of this world is, on account of the general connection of things, a natural sign of the thing caused, and the latter is a natural sign of each of its causes that is real.   (p. 36)

Not only is the effect a sign of the cause, without which it would not exist, but the cause is also a sign of the effect, "since one," as Meier writes, "can reason from the reality of the cause to the reality of the thing caused" (p. 36). This extension of the meaning of sign and signifying connection is carried forward in §72:

If a real relation exists between two things, then that thing which stands in a certain relation to the other thing is a natural sign of the thing to which the first thing relates, and vice versa [...].   (p. 38)

Meier not only interprets causal relations as a relation between sign and signified — indeed, one that is reversible, such that the cause is also a sign of the effect and not just the other way around — he also views the relation between end and means, and even model and copy, as a signifying connection, again one that is reversible. To understand this way of looking at things, we must distinguish between the idea of pervasive connection and the view that this connection is a signifying one. The former idea accords completely with the philosophy of Leibniz to which Meier explicitly refers when he says "in this world, because it is the best, there exists the very greatest degree of general, signifying connection which is possible in a world" (p. 18). God appears in this view as the creator of the world, but not as its ruler. The world itself assumes responsibility, so to speak, for its proper functioning; the umbilical cord linking it to its creator has been cut. But because it was created by God and bears witness to God, without his being able, after the creation, to intervene and take responsibility for running it properly, the world must have been organized from the very outset as the best of all possible worlds.

It does not matter for our purposes whether Meier's notion that the functional connection which constitutes the world is a signifying connection was also influenced by Leibniz — that is, by his previously mentioned general theory of characteristic — or by other authors — Geldsetzer mentions John Locke, in whose *Essay Concerning Human Understanding* (1690) knowledge is divided into the physical, the practical, and the semiotic (i.e., a knowledge of signs).[7] Meier's pansemiotics, his extension of hermeneutics to include the explanation of nature (*explicatio naturae*), is of consequence for the hermeneutics of artificial signs, i.e., for that portion of Meier's general theory of interpretation which is a hermeneutics in our sense of the term, only insofar as the characteristics of natural signs recur, with certain qualifications, in artificial signs, and insofar as interpretation of the latter takes its rules, again with certain qualifications, from the former, and — this is the decisive point — insofar as the relationship between the interpreter and the author of the text to be interpreted takes as its model the attitude required toward the creator of the world. Meier's theory of artificial signs and their interpretation is a modification of his theory of natural signs and their interpretation. For this reason we will first take up the latter.

It follows from the premise borrowed from Leibniz about this world being the best (Meier suppresses the end of the phrase, "of all possible worlds") not only that the "very greatest degree of general, signifying connection" (p. 18) exists in it, but also, and more significantly for the hermeneutics of artificial signs, that "the natural signs in this world are the most perfect" (§37, p. 19). God is the creator of the signifying connection in this world; every natural sign is an effect of God. "In respect to God," Meier writes, "every natural sign is an arbitrary [*willkürlich*] sign and thus a consequence of the wisest choice and the best intention" (§38, p. 19). If a signifying connection exists between cause and effect, i.e., if the effect is always a sign of the cause, then natural as well as artificial signs are signs of their originators and resemble them insofar as this resemblance is not thwarted by some other factor, such as the author's folly in seizing on the wrong sign.

Natural signs, by contrast, are the consequence of the wisest choice and the best intention; here all of God's perfections flow together. But what constitutes the perfection of natural signs? §40 describes it as follows: "The more fruitful [*fruchtbar*], the greater or more dignified a

[7] Ibid., p. xvii.

72

sign, the clearer, the more appropriate, precise, and practical a sign, the more perfect it is" (p. 20). Since these perfections of natural signs are also characteristic of artificial signs, although only within the framework of the modification just noted, we need to examine more closely what Meier means by them.

The fruitfulness of a sign (copia, foecunditas signi) is that perfection of the sign by virtue of which it is possible to recognize the reality of many things from it [...]. Thus, to the extent that a sign signifies either many meanings which are coordinated or subordinated to one another, or many aspects of one meaning, to that extent it is a fruitful sign. (§41, p. 21)

The magnitude of a sign (magnitudo signi) is that perfection of the sign by virtue of which it signifies great things [...]. Great meanings have either a physical or moral greatness, the latter of which are called dignified objects. A thing has physical greatness when it is the cause of great consequences or is the consequence of great causes or a whole constituted of many and great parts. A thing has dignity when it is not opposed to the higher and nobler virtues but rather accords with them and fosters them. (§47, pp. 24f.)

The clarity of a sign (claritas signi) is that perfection of the sign by virtue of which it itself, and through it also its meaning, can be sufficiently distinguished from all other things. (§50, p. 26)

The truth[8] *of a sign (veritas signi)* is that perfection of the sign by virtue of which the true reality of the thing signified can be correctly recognized from it. *A false sign (signum falsum)* is either a sign which has no meaning at all or one whose meaning was not real, is not real, and will not be real in this world, or one whose meaning is in fact real but can be discerned from the sign only by means of a false perception. (§57, pp. 30f.)

The precision of a sign (certitudo signi) is that perfection of the sign by virtue of which it is certain that it is not just a sign but also a sign of a thing which is characterized as having specific qualities and which really exists in this world in the way claimed. (§59, p. 31)

The natural sign is further defined, negatively, as not being ambiguous [*zweydeutig*]:

An ambiguous sign (signum ambiguum, amphibolicum) is a sign which has several meanings. The more meanings a sign has, the more varied these are, and the more they are in opposition to one another, and the more equal the ease and the difficulty with which these meanings can be recognized in the sign, the greater is the ambiguity of the sign and the more difficult it is to recognize a certain specific meaning from the sign. Therefore, natural signs are not ambiguous. Any interpretation of natural signs is, accordingly, false

---

[8] I.e., the correctness or appropriateness.

if its truth would entail that natural signs are ambiguous. Indeed, the greater the ambiguity of natural signs resulting from such an interpretation would be, the more such an interpretation would be repugnant to the hermeneutic reverence for God. (§55, p. 29)

What Meier means when he holds that natural signs, as the most perfect, are at the same time the *most practical*, becomes evident in §65. Here we read:

The life of natural signs (*vita signorum naturalium*) is that perfection of signs by virtue of which they mean something the knowledge of which is useful to people, for example, when natural signs are necessary to people to achieve their true goals, necessary to promote their welfare; when they serve to promote virtue and obstruct vice; and when, generally, their interpretation is necessary and useful to people when they otherwise wish to act as true perfection requires. [...] That natural signs are the most vivid [*lebendig*] is also explained by the fact that everything that exists in the best world promotes religion, the highest bliss of spirits, and thus also virtue. (pp. 34f.)

Meier uses the word "practical," then, in the sense in which we also encounter it in the title of Kant's ethical philosophy, his *Critique of Practical Reason*. Practical is what has to do with things as they should be. When Meier calls natural signs, as the most practical, also the most vivid, we are reminded of the vivid knowledge discussed by Chladenius. Knowledge is vivid if it results in an act of will: to this extent a sign which brings about vivid knowledge is "practical" in the sense just noted. Whereas Chladenius spoke of vivid knowledge as a *possible* application, a possible mediated sense of a passage or text, however, Meier posits the perfection resulting from such vivid knowledge as the defining feature of natural signs. Thus everything hinges on the question of how he views the relationship between artificial signs, those, that is to say, of which texts are composed, and natural signs.

One could imagine a theory of artificial, or man-made, signs for which the theory of natural – one could also say divine – signs just outlined would be a counter-theory. One could imagine a theory which described the perfections of natural signs only to stress, over against this radiant background, the imperfections of artificial signs, of signs that would be barren and meager, incapable of guaranteeing correctness and certainty, unequipped to influence the way we live. Such a pessimistic theory is conceivable, but not for a philosopher of the Enlightenment who was a follower of Leibniz. This world of ours was for him the best; no divine world could be contrasted to it. Are then artificial signs perfect like the natural ones? Yes and no. Artificial signs are chosen by human beings as natural signs are by God. The latter are the result of "the wisest choice and the best intention" (§38, p. 19). This cannot on the whole be postulated of human beings.

A shrewd and rational originator of signs [i.e., the author] will use those intentional signs that signify things which are not only as perfect as possible in their own right but also accord best with his own perfections and with the perfections of those for whom he signifies them [i.e., the reader].

(§86, p. 45)

If this is the case, if the signs have been chosen shrewdly (§84, p. 44), then they have a good meaning. If, on the other hand, they have been chosen foolishly, "then they have either no meaning at all or a bad one, or they signify a good meaning in a poor way" (p. 44). Such signs, however, should not be interpreted at all. Only if it first becomes apparent in the course of interpretation that they "were chosen foolishly" do they deserve to be the object of interpretation (§85, p. 44). What this means is that the interpreter does not set about interpretation in an unbiased way in order to inquire into the meaning of a sign, whereby it is supposed to become evident whether it has been chosen foolishly or shrewdly. Rather, interpretation proceeds on the assumption that signs have been chosen wisely until this is proven false. That is, the interpretation itself uses this expectation as a criterion; if the expectation is disappointed, if the sign proves to have been chosen foolishly, then this is not so much a finding of the interpretation as evidence that the interpretation should be terminated, that it should never have been undertaken in the first place.

Meier expresses these ideas – which are not only of the greatest consequence for his hermeneutics but may still be found, in modified form, in our own interpretive practice – in the concept of "hermeneutic fairness":

Hermeneutic fairness (aequitas hermeneutica) is the tendency of the interpreter to hold those meanings to be hermeneutically true that best accord with the perfections of the creator of the signs, until the opposite be proven. When considered with respect to God, this fairness can be called *hermeneutic reverence for God (reverentia erga deum hermeneutica).* (§39, p. 20)

As a fundamental principle of the interpretation of natural signs, this rests on a concept of God the correctness of which does not have to be proven by hermeneutics, for it is a given. The situation is different when this principle is applied to the interpretation of arbitrary signs.

The interpretation of such signs would have to be preceded by a conceptualization of the author and his perfections that was analogous to this concept of God. Meier did not overlook this. He writes:

> An interpreter who interprets arbitrary signs must hold that meaning to be hermeneutically correct which best accords with the perfections of the originator of those signs, until the opposite becomes apparent. Consequently he must acquaint himself, as far as possible, with the perfections of the originator of the signs before he sets about interpretation of them.
>
> (§95, p. 49)

The parenthetical "as far as possible" points, to be sure, to the difficulties which will repeatedly be encountered in attaining the knowledge of an author that is supposed to precede interpretation of his work, but not to the fundamental problem associated therewith. For the question is, of course, how the interpreter is to become acquainted with an author's perfections if not through his text or texts. Homer and Shakespeare, whom we know solely through their works, or better still, whom we know only *as* the authors of their works, are from the hermeneutic point of view borderline cases rather than exceptions. Knowledge about the person who is also the author of a work, however we obtain it besides through the work, can certainly contribute to understanding the work, but we still must not overlook the difference between X as a person and X as an author any more than we do the difference between author and work.

These, to be sure, are insights which are historically conditioned in two senses: first, the relationship that exists between author and work is subject to historical change; second, as the concept of literature changes over time so too does that of the relationship between work and author. If we wished to indulge in a terrible oversimplification, we could say that the goal of interpretation in the eighteenth century was knowledge of the subject matter presented in the work; in the nineteenth century, knowledge of the author; and in the twentieth century, knowledge of the work. The interest of the eighteenth-century hermeneuticist was far from limited to works; he never doubted the possibility of getting to know an author's perfections through other means even *before* interpreting his works. Thus he never encountered the hermeneutic circle that for us, as already for nineteenth-century hermeneuticists, lies concealed there. When we scrutinize Meier's postulate of hermeneutic fairness, the first thing to become problematic on account of the historically conditioned change in the telos of interpretation is that those meanings which best accord with the author's perfections must be regarded as true until proven otherwise. For these perfections only reveal themselves in the course of interpretation.

A further feature of the postulate of fairness that proves to be historically conditioned is Meier's material definition of the perfections to be attributed to an author or his chosen signs. These perfections are borrowed from the theory of natural signs, which in turn is informed by the concept of God in Leibniz's philosophy. From the standpoint of contemporary hermeneutics we must not only ask, therefore, whether familiarity with an author ought to precede interpretation of his work and whether we should attribute to the signs that constitute the work perfections corresponding to those of its author, until the opposite be proven; we must also ask what the perfections of the signs consist in.

I have already mentioned that in the transition from natural to artificial signs in Meier's work it is not the concept and the material definition of the perfections themselves that change, but only the certainty of their givenness. An interpreter who interprets arbitrary signs must "hold that meaning to be hermeneutically true which is just as good, grand, rich in content, true, clear, precise, and practical as it can be, until the opposite becomes apparent" (§94, p. 49). If we now disregard the postulate of hermeneutic fairness itself and examine the normative characteristics that Meier ascribes to arbitrary signs, we can divide them into two groups. One set pertains to an aspect of content and the other to a formal aspect. Given that even a contemporary semiology might go beyond the descriptive and focus on ideals, we will not reject Meier's perfections out of hand, but instead will have to examine them individually and analyze their presuppositions.

Among the perfections which pertain to content are the size and the ethical aspect [*das Praktische*] of signs. The assumption that the signs of a text to be interpreted designate physically grand, morally grand, i.e., dignified, objects and make possible a kind of knowledge which serves to promote virtue and obstruct vice — an assumption that is not to be abandoned until the opposite becomes apparent (and then merely in the specific case at hand, not in general) — stands or falls with the view that the world is perfectly constructed. This is sufficiently obvious to need no elaboration. It is otherwise with the formal perfections. They imply that signs must be (1) "fruitful," i.e., "signify many meanings which are coordinated or subordinated to one another" (§41, p. 21); (2) "clear," i.e., distinguished from other signs and capable of guaranteeing the distinction between their meaning and other meanings (§50, p. 26); (3) "true," i.e., bring about knowledge of the true reality of the thing signified (§57, p. 30); and, finally, (4) "precise," i.e., point unambiguously to the intended meaning (§59, pp. 31f.).

When the perfections of a sign are evaluated today from a functional point of view, clarity and precision are certain to be counted among them. It will probably be otherwise with respect to the truth and fruitfulness of signs. Meier means two things by the truth of a sign: first, the sign must have a meaning; second, the meaning must have reality in this world. Now, whereas the existence of a meaning is essential to the definition of the sign, it seems highly questionable whether a sign, in signifying, also reveals the "true reality of the thing signified" (§57, p. 30). The validity of this claim would have to be examined within the framework of semiology. With regard to the fruitfulness of the sign, finally, we must first note the tension between this postulate and the requirement that the sign be precise, i.e., univocal. A sign should have "many meanings," to be sure, but these must be "coordinated or subordinated to one another" (§41, p. 21). The interconnections among the different meanings thus preclude ambiguity: rather than ambiguity, it is, instead, complexity of meaning which results. If we were to evaluate this last characteristic of the sign from a purely functional point of view, we would hardly call it a *perfection*. From an aesthetic point of view, however, the inner complexity of the sign may be considered a positive attribute – by comparison to which both pure univocality and the sort of multiplicity of meaning in which the various potential meanings are either unrelated to one another or even exclude one another must appear as imperfections.

Now, when Meier posits the fruitfulness of the sign as one of its perfections, it might seem that he is giving expression to a notion of poetic language much more familiar to the late nineteenth and twentieth centuries than to the eighteenth century. This contradiction can be resolved by recognizing that Meier was not interested in a specific aesthetic quality of language when he formulated the postulate of fruitfulness. This quality found its way into his discussion of artificial signs by way of a direct transference of the perfections attributable to natural signs, i.e., to things existing in the world. The fruitfulness of natural signs, however, is nothing other than an expression of the multiplicity of interconnections that constitute the world and – as has been shown to be the case in Leibniz – make God dispensable for all practical purposes. If we wish to retain fruitfulness as a postulate in a semiology and hermeneutics that are free of these presuppositions, then we must assume a poetics that is anchored not beyond but *in* literary history. The hermeneutics such a poetics requires will reveal itself to be historically determined as well.

The postulate of hermeneutic fairness, on the other hand, will need to be reformulated in terms of our own conceptions and on the basis of our hermeneutic practice. Does the recognition of, say, clarity and precision as desirable qualities of artificial signs mean that in interpretation they must be assumed to be present until proven otherwise? Certainly not. Yet in a modified form the postulate of hermeneutic fairness does appear to be familiar to contemporary hermeneutic practice. This can probably be shown in detail only within the context of a comparative analysis of understanding and criticism such as has become current in the last decades, thanks largely to Walter Benjamin's distinction between criticism and commentary at the beginning of his essay on *Die Wahlverwandtschaften* [*Elective Affinities*].[9] If we look at how understanding actually proceeds, we find that hermeneutic fairness does not so much involve our assuming the presence of qualities until proven otherwise as it does our querying the text for the presence of these qualities. We certainly do not take them as given, sight unseen – as if this world were the best – but as a potentiality they nevertheless condition understanding, for we proceed by asking whether the possibilities are actualized in a given text. One reason interpretations are historically conditioned is that the questions they pose depend on the intentions they impute to texts. But it is undoubtedly one of the most difficult problems of contemporary hermeneutics to bring together the element of affirmation, which would *seem*, as a working hypothesis, to be essential to the process of understanding, with the critical attitude of not letting the wool be pulled over our eyes, which we feel obliged to adopt as long as this is not the best of all possible worlds.

[9] Walter Benjamin, "Goethes Wahlverwandtschaften," in Benjamin, *Gesammelte Schriften*, vol. 1, pt. 1, ed. Rolf Tiedemann and Hermann Schweppenhäuser (Frankfurt am Main, 1974), pp. 125f.

Meier, II

As the class of signs includes, besides artificial signs — which alone we would call signs today — natural signs as well, that is, everything that exists in the world, and as the connection which governs them, according to Meier, is one of sign and signified, the *interpretatio scriptorum* becomes a special case of *interpretatio naturae*. The interpretation of literary works is governed by the law of hermeneutic fairness just as is the interpretation of the creation by the law of hermeneutic reverence for God. Fairness is distinguished from reverence in that it does not require us to believe in the perfections of work and author — by contrast with those of creation and creator — but only to regard them as given until proven otherwise. For the rules of secular hermeneutics — whose opposite was now no longer biblical exegesis but *interpretatio naturae* in the Baroque sense (Leibniz, upon whom Meier builds, can certainly be considered a philosopher of the Baroque) — there are two chief consequences of the postulate of hermeneutic fairness which allow us to measure the influence of this postulate: (1) recourse to the author in interpretation; and (2) a hierarchy of the different *sensus* — i.e., of proper and improper meaning as well as of straightforward and mediated meaning.

Recourse to the author is not something which would uniquely characterize Meier's hermeneutics. In its origins in antiquity interpretation aimed at determining the author's meaning. This is clear in the case of grammatical interpretation, which assumes that the historical change to which language is subject prevents the word from functioning as a sign of what the author wished to express. It is less clear in the case of allegorical interpretation, whose originators can hardly have been aware of the discrepancy between intention and allegorical exegesis when, for instance, they placed the stories of the Old Testament in the context of the story of the life and sufferings of Christ presented in the New Testament. In short, although the view that authorial intention is a criterion of interpretation pervades the entire history of hermeneutics, and the turn away from this view – in, say, Valéry and George – must be seen as an exception, the motives for propounding this view and the degree of prominence it has been assigned have changed historically.

Between Chladenius and Meier we can already see a marked difference on this issue. Chladenius, whose primary orientation lies in the psychology of effects, comes to the conclusion that complete understanding of a passage need by no means coincide with the author's intention, and he has recourse to authorial intention only to achieve certainty of interpretation – whereby the criterion emerges as a principle of classification to determine which of the various elements of the complete understanding accord with the author's intention. The principle of hermeneutic fairness, on the other hand, which is the highest law in Meier's theory of interpretation, has recourse to the author and his intentions not as a consequence but as a precondition. Because interpretation is the interpretation of signs, yet signs are not only signs of the thing signified but – in accordance with the theory of natural signs which rests on the analogy between the perfections of the best of all possible worlds and the perfections of its creator – also signs of their originator, the postulate of recourse to the author exists, as it were, independently of the task of interpretation, simply as the postulate of fairness, which is modeled on reverence for God. Interpretation itself, the understanding of works, is subordinated to this postulate not in order to guarantee certainty of interpretation, as in Chladenius, but in order to be able to understand the works, as far as possible – i.e., until proven otherwise – as signs of their author, as confirmation of his presumed perfections.

This assumption on the part of the interpreter ought not to be unfounded, of course, and in fact Meier demands that the interpreter "acquaint himself with the perfections of the signs before he sets about interpretation of them – insofar as this is possible" (§95, p. 49), he adds with good reason, by way of qualification. That authorial intention is the criterion of interpretation follows from §112 where we learn:

The sense of a discourse is that series of interconnected ideas which the author wishes to signify through the discourse. Accordingly, no meaning and no series of meanings which the author did not intend belongs to the sense, or constitutes the sense of his discourse, even though he could have signified these through his discourse, indeed, even though he perhaps would have done better to have signified them through his discourse. (p. 62)

What is relevant to interpretation according to Meier is the meaning of the sign only insofar as it was intended by the author. Meaning and intention are equated with each other where we read in §117 that the *"hermeneutically true meaning* [is] the intention for the sake of which the creator of the sign uses it" (p. 9). The signs themselves most assuredly can also mean something else, and this other meaning may even be closer to them than the one the author intended; nonetheless, the meaning the author intended is the single legitimate goal of interpretation. The interpreter's understanding and the author's intention must coincide. §128 states:

He *understands words and discourse* (*intelligere vocabula et orationem*) who discerns in them their meanings and sense. The interpreter understands words and discourse accordingly. Accordingly the author and his interpreter think one and the same thing. The interpreter who thinks none of the same things the author was thinking does not understand the author at all; but the interpreter who does not think exactly the same things the author was thinking does not understand the author correctly. (pp. 69f.)

Now, if the author himself interprets what he has written, this constitutes an "authentic interpretation," and whoever interprets a discourse "contrary to the authentic interpretation [...] is an unfair interpreter in that he assumes that the author either spoke and wrote without understanding or did not understand himself" (§138, p. 75). Only when it "becomes evident that the author changed his meaning and had a different one from the one he uttered and a different one from the one he interpreted his words to mean" (§138, p. 76), may the interpreter deviate from the author's self-interpretation. Just as it does not occur to Meier, when he requires us to acquaint ourselves with the author's perfections before beginning an interpretation, to explain how this is to be accomplished, neither does it occur to him here to ask whether a change of meaning, introduced between the composition of a text and the author's explication of it, cannot after all only be inferred through interpretation itself. For even when such a change in the author's thinking is documented by other sources, this does not mean that in explaining what he wrote earlier, he will necessarily revise the earlier intention. On the contrary, it is only by interpreting the text, by comparison with the "authentic interpretation" (§136, p. 74) – which thus in turn must be interpreted – that the relationship between the two can be determined.

That Meier did not take note of the hidden problems in his theory of interpretation is all the more remarkable considering the fact that his terminology registers the very classificatory distinctions from which they stem. He distinguishes, first of all, between hermeneutic principles and hermeneutic aids and, secondly, between internal and external hermeneutic principles.

Hermeneutic principles (principia hermeneutica) are principles that govern interpretation; *hermeneutic aids (subsidia hermeneutica)*, however, are tools that facilitate and foster the recognition of meaning on the basis of hermeneutic principles. Whoever grasps meanings solely by means of hermeneutic aids accomplishes anything but an interpretation. Consequently, an interpreter who wishes to interpret in a reasonable and logical fashion must derive his interpretation from the hermeneutic principles. [...] *Internal hermeneutic principles* are parts of the signs which are to be interpreted; and the remaining principles which are distinct from these are called *external hermeneutic principles*. The sign itself that is to be interpreted and its relation to the meaning are internal hermeneutic principles.   (§21—22, pp. 11—12)

The hermeneutic principles from which the interpretation is deduced may be sufficient or insufficient. A hermeneutic proof is itself either sufficient or insufficient depending on whether it is supported by sufficient or insufficient principles. The sufficient proof makes the meaning hermeneutically certain, the insufficient proof merely makes it hermeneutically probable. That Meier no longer postulates certainty of interpretation undoubtedly represents an advance over Chladenius for hermeneutic theory. While Chladenius, despite his insight into the projection of meaning beyond intention, insists on the certainty of interpretation and grounds this on so uncertain a basis as the coincidence of intention and understanding, Meier acknowledges this shortcoming of hermeneutic reasoning which defines and distinguishes it from logical reasoning.

The greatest possible hermeneutic certainty is never totally without fear of its opposite, consequently it is never an apodictic certainty. [...] Whoever expects a mathematical demonstration from an interpreter and commentator, therefore, is expecting something impossible and unreasonable.

(§242, pp. 125f.)

If the interpreter wishes to argue the truth of a meaning on the basis of insufficient evidence, he must "set forth the hermeneutic probability of it" (§243). This is accomplished by weighing the reasons that speak for and those that speak against a particular interpretation.

What does Meier mean then by hermeneutic aids and hermeneutic principles? He raises the issue of hermeneutic aids in the context of discussing "literal meaning" [*büchstäblicher Sinn*]. This can be discerned, according to Meier, from the discourse itself without reference to the author, that is, from the individual words, expressions, and syntactic structures. Usage determines what the words, expressions, and syntactic structures of a particular language have meant and can still mean. Usage is thus a hermeneutic principle from which the interpreter may derive the literal sense. One of the tools which – to recall the definition to mind – facilitates and fosters the recognition of meaning on the basis of the hermeneutic principle of usage is the dictionary. It contains not only the usage of words but also their etymology, homonymy, and synonymy.

The meanings of derivative words are determined by derivation from their root words. Thus the interpreter can discern the literal meaning from etymology. – The homonymy of a word includes all the meanings that a word tends to have as a result of usage of the word; and the meaning of a word can be discerned from another word which means the same thing but is better known. Thus the interpreter can learn the literal meanings from homonymy and synonymy. (§145, pp. 78f.)

The second hermeneutic aid, next to the dictionary, is grammar. It teaches us, as we read in §148, "the declensions of individual words and the resulting changes in their meaning, syntactic structures and the resulting meanings of individual phrases, and the changes in these" (p. 80). Although dictionary and grammar function, as we see, as suppliers of hermeneutic principles, Meier insists that they are not themselves hermeneutic principles but simply aids. One should beware of:

(1) considering a dictionary a hermeneutic principle, either in theory or in practice. For even if one assumes and may assume that its author has not erred, still he could have erred, so an interpreter will be too hasty in his judgment if he accepts a literal meaning merely on account of the dictionary; (2) accepting everything the dictionary states to be true because one is prejudiced by appearances. (§147, p. 79)

Following this is the statement that with regard to grammar the interpreter must "avoid everything he has to guard against with the dictionary" (§148, p. 80), and §149 reads in lapidary style: "What we have noted regarding the dictionary and grammar also applies to the whole of philology" (p. 80).

When we read the thesis that philology is not a hermeneutic principle, that an interpretation cannot therefore be deduced from it, we are reminded of our earlier reflections on the lines "Denck' ich nur dran, mein Herz möcht' da für Boßheit reißen" ["If I so much as think of it, my heart is torn with malice"] from Goethe's *The Lover's Caprice*. We tried to show[1] that the interpretation is not provided by the dictionary information that *Boßheit* [malice] once also meant *Ärger* [anger], *Wut* [rage], that the interpretation depends rather on the insight that (and why) the word means *Ärger* here and not *Boßheit* – an insight we owe to interpretation. Thus even at the time the dictionary could have been characterized only as a hermeneutic aid, not as a hermeneutic principle.

But this thesis has neither the same meaning nor the same consequences for Meier. If dictionary, grammar, and philology do not count as hermeneutic principles in his theory of interpretation, that is not because usage itself, about which they inform us, is not a hermeneutic principle, but only because the information they provide about usage can be false. It is inconsistent, and also slightly amusing, when he warns us expressly against "accepting everything the dictionary states to be true because one is prejudiced by appearances," for the same standard should hold for the use of the dictionary as for interpretation: namely, the postulate of hermeneutic fairness, the disposition to accept a piece of information as correct until it is proven false. But it is more important to note that all of Meier's skepticism is reserved for the issue of correctness, while the idea that usage, etymology, homonymy, and synonymy might be problematic as hermeneutic principles is alien to him. Although we ought not to criticize an eighteenth-century hermeneuticist for disregarding facts of linguistic history that did not become objects of research before the nineteenth century, following the development of modern philology as an historical discipline, we should nevertheless note that while etymology elucidates the derivation of words, it does not necessarily also elucidate the meaning of the derivative words. For just as every word is subject to semantic change over time, this is often associated with derivation – that is, with compounding, i.e., expansion by prefixes and suffixes – so a return to the origins of the root will invariably miss the meaning of the derivative word. Thus, etymology does not furnish insight into the meaning of a derivative word, it merely enables us to follow the process by which the meaning changed. The same applies to homonymy and synonymy. If in this regard, too, the dictionary can be seen only as a hermeneutic aid, not

---

[1] See Chapter 2, pp. 23–4.

as a hermeneutic principle, this is not just because the homonymy and synonymy given in the dictionary are sometimes false. On the contrary, even correct homonymy and synonymy could not guarantee a correct interpretation. When Meier maintains that the "meaning of a word can be discerned from another word which means the same thing but is better known" (§146, p. 79), he overlooks the fact that in order to establish synonymy one must already know the meaning of the word to be interpreted.

The dictionary is here only a moderately useful aid, not so much because of possible errors as because it records the possible synonymies in a given language, but not those relevant in a given case. That is to say, only when understanding of a word fails because the word is unknown can a synonym provided by the dictionary facilitate interpretation, not when, owing to its ambiguity, the word requires interpretation. For the synonyms listed in the dictionary presuppose this ambiguity, whereas in interpretation only *those* synonyms can be a hermeneutic principle which relate to the meaning of the inherently ambiguous word that is actualized in a given passage.

The dictionary informs us – to use Saussure's terminology – about the *langue*; the passage to be interpreted, however, is an instance of *parole*. The step from *langue* to *parole*, as the process of understanding a passage may be designated, the recapitulation of the actualizing process, is thus indebted to the dictionary, as also to grammar and philology as a whole, only for providing knowledge of the possibilities: dictionary and grammar can prove an interpretation false because it imputes a relationship between *langue* and *parole*, an actualization which is not possible; but dictionary and grammar cannot show *which* of a number of possible steps is the correct one, *which* of a number of possible actualizations, if repeated, will capture the correct meaning in a given case. In this respect neither etymology nor homonymy and synonymy are hermeneutic principles; on the contrary, interpretation has its principle within itself, in the production of evidence.

Closely associated with the problem of homonymy and synonymy and their hermeneutic function is the problem of parallel passages. Where the former are included in dictionaries, the latter constitute, as it were, a work's own individual dictionary. The concordance – such as we know and use for the Bible, for classical authors, and increasingly for more recent authors as well – the index of passages, that is, in which a word occurs, is, however, only one half of this imaginary dictionary. Since the concordance proceeds from the word, the sign, and not from what is signified, it shows only the homonymies, not the synonymies as well. But both are equally relevant – because of the internal consistency of the hermeneutic system, in fact – for the theory of parallel passages known to eighteenth-century interpretative theory.

Parallel passages (*loca parallela*) are utterances or parts of utterances that are similar to the text at hand. They are thus similar to the text with respect either to the words or the meaning and sense, or in both respects. The first comprise *word parallelism* (*parallelismus verbalis*); the second, *object parallelism* (*parallelismus realis*); and the third, *mixed parallelism* (*parallelismus mixtus*).

(§151, p. 81)

Whereas word parallelism enables us to recognize homonymy, synonymy can be recognized through object parallelism. Just as Meier perceives a hermeneutic principle in homonymy and synonymy, so too in word- and object-parallelism. The parallel passage method taught in the eighteenth century differs from today's practice first of all in that it recognizes not only word identity but also object identity. It hopes for illumination of an obscure passage not merely from passages in which the same word is used, but also from those in which the same object is designated by a different word. Here, of course, we confront the same question we met with before when we had to consider whether synonymy and homonymy were to be regarded as hermeneutic principles. Word parallelism can of course be established on the basis of the identity of words; but whether the word has the same meaning in both passages, whether the parallel passage is suited to illuminate the meaning of the passage to be interpreted, is never settled at the outset, but is decided only in the course of interpretation.[2] Even more questionable is the value of object parallelism as evidence. Since it presupposes the nonidentity of signs and the identity only of what is signified, the question arises as to how these could possibly be determined prior to interpretation. Meier's art of interpretation not only ignores this question, it privileges object parallelism over word parallelism.

The more similar parallel passages are to each other and the more they are connected to each other, the easier it is to recognize from the one passage the

---

[2] See Peter Szondi, "On Textual Understanding," in Szondi, *On Textual Understanding and Other Essays*, tr. Harvey Mendelsohn (Minneapolis, 1986), pp. 3–22.

literal meaning of the other, and the less insufficient they are as hermeneutic principles. Hence, object parallelism is a better hermeneutic principle than word parallelism, and mixed parallelism is better still.   (§154, pp. 82f.)

This is comprehensible only in the light of an orientation to subject matter.[3] This orientation informs Meier's hermeneutics as well.

Whereas, in keeping with its function as a compendium, Meier's *Versuch einer allgemeinen Auslegungskunst* does not go into any details of the parallel passage method and Meier contents himself with the observation that parallel passages are insufficient hermeneutic principles, we find a number of observations on this method in Chladenius' *Einleitung*.[4] Like Meier, Chladenius was familiar with both word parallelism and object parallelism; in fact, he points out further types of parallelism which are defined by the identity not of the word or the object but of the intention or of the relationship between words (§300). An example of the latter is the purely formal relationship between two words that a comparative analysis of the genitive metaphors in a poem or in a poet's opus would reveal. Parallel passages, Chladenius writes, must

> often give us the strongest light for the discovery of the true sense of obscure passages; even more, however, do they serve to inform us of objects about which we must learn from books. We receive clear and detailed concepts from them; they lead us to knowledge of the causes and interconnections of things and put us in a position to fashion a system out of scattered truths.
>
> (§300, pp. 176f.)

This use of parallel passages, which is not really a hermeneutic use, is familiar to us as well — we need only think of Eisler's Kant lexicon, Glockner's Hegel lexicon, the index to *Being and Time*. As far as the hermeneutic function of parallel passages is concerned, however, Chladenius makes several points and distinctions which are also of importance to contemporary hermeneutics — even disregarding the fact that parallel passages show us nothing external to interpretation or independent of it which could serve as a basis for interpretation, but rather something which needs to be incorporated into it.

First of all, Chladenius refers to the problem we encountered in Meier's discussion of "authentic interpretation," or self-interpretation: the possibility that the author has changed his views in the interim between two parallel passages:

---

[3] See the discussion of Chladenius' orientation to subject matter, Chapter 4, pp. 43ff.
[4] According to Szondi's inventory: §300, §304, §393, §394, §398, §502.

Since the author of a text does not write the passages all at once, but at various different times, since he can have changed his mind in the meantime, one ought not indiscriminately to view the parallel passages of an author as belonging together, but only those which he wrote without changing his mind. It follows from this that what a person wrote in many books, indeed even what he wrote in different places within one long work, ought not to be gathered together indiscriminately as one single explanation by the author. For as the completion of a long work requires a great deal of time, one can present contradictory opinions in a single book, one of which we agree with in the beginning, and another later on. (§304, p. 179)

However much to the point this statement may be, however necessary it is to make it, since in practice the use of parallel passages, now as then, is relatively uncritical, criticism ought not to restrict itself to the question of whether the same or a different intention underlies ostensibly parallel passages. We must also question the premise that it is possible to determine prior to or independently of the interpretation of two passages whether or not they derive from the same intention.

The thesis that contradictory opinions may be present in a longer work because of the length of time required to complete it leads Chladenius to a second important point: the genre distinctions which here too hermeneutics must take into account.

Books written according to the mathematical way of teaching have the advantage over all others that one cannot properly present something in them that is contradictory, nor bring forth differing opinions either. For even if one should change one's mind during composition, one would, by virtue of this method, necessarily have to change the preceding parts as well. With other books, by contrast, it is not only possible to contradict oneself, it is also useful, in an emergency, to have an escape if one is challenged on an opinion; indeed, to some it may even seem like *galanterie* to show a certain skepticism in one's writings. (§304, pp. 179f.)

Whatever function may be ascribed to the contradiction between two passages of a work, the important thing is that Chladenius discusses this limitation on the validity of the parallel passage method. In what textbook of literary criticism from our own century will we find anything comparable? And it is no less important that he recognized that the possibility of such contradictions is dependent upon the genre, the *modus dicendi*, of the work in which they occur. That we must go beyond his distinctions and explanations goes without saying, for we shall not want to regard the contradictoriness or inconsistency of a work merely as the result of a lengthy period of composition, but rather will view the temporal factor as something that may have been incorporated into the work. Where the passage of time is not merely an object for the work (narrated time) or a means of expression external to its intention (time of narration), where instead the idea of the work really only comes into its own through its projection outwards, its stepping forth into the realm of temporal diversity, in such cases the work should be interpreted only as a process, whereby each passage must be explicated with a view to its positional value. This relationship between a work's structure and temporality is among the questions relevant to an historical theory of literary forms, of which we have only the beginnings – for instance in Lukács' *Theory of the Novel* and Benjamin's book on *The Origin of German Tragic Drama*. Adorno's *Philosophy of Modern Music* also contains important observations on this problematic.[a] Only on the basis of the findings of such an historical theory of forms, which also does justice to the phenomenon of a work's temporality [*Werkzeit*], will hermeneutics be able to carry forward Chladenius' criticism of the parallel passage method as an inquiry into the conditions of the possibility of interpretation by means of parallel passages.

A third way of "misusing parallel passages" is

when one attempts to deduce the meaning of metaphorical words in one place from the metaphorical use of the very same word in other places. One knows that one can learn the common meaning of words from their use on different occasions; from this rule, which one takes to be more general than it really is, one concludes that because the word was taken in this figurative sense in one place, or in several, it must assume that same sense in another passage as well.   (§396, p. 281)

And after he has illustrated the possibility of misinterpretation that arises in this manner, Chladenius lays down the rule

that the figurative meaning of a word in a given passage cannot be determined with certitude from another passage where the word is also used but for another thing. For a word can be used in the figurative sense on diverse occasions, and with every use a new concept emerges. Thus, even if I know that the word has this particular figurative sense in this particular place, it does not follow that it must have this very sense in another place as well.   (§398, p. 283)

[a] Georg Lukács, *Theory of the Novel*, tr. Anna Bostock (Cambridge, Mass., 1971); Walter Benjamin, *The Origin of German Tragic Drama*; Theodor W. Adorno, *Philosophy of Modern Music*, tr. Anne G. Mitchell and Wesley V. Blomster (New York, 1973).

Here too it must be regretted that contemporary literary theory considers itself above elucidating the questions that the pre-philosophical hermeneutics of the eighteenth century took up and answered in terms of rules which, *as* rules, are possibly no longer valid, the content of which, however, thereby becomes all the more relevant. The reason why the rules formulated by Chladenius need to be revised for contemporary hermeneutics is that they proceed from the metaphorical use of a word without taking into account the fact that the observation that a word is being used metaphorically is itself already part of the interpretation. The latter thus cannot be made dependent upon whether metaphorical usage is or is not present.

Once again the question arises: what are the consequences of the postulate of hermeneutic fairness, as defined in Meier's theory of interpretation, for the hermeneutic decision about whether we are to assume the presence in a passage of proper or improper (i.e., metaphorical) meaning, and further, of straightforward or mediated meaning? Meier attributes a type of perfection to artificial signs as possible signs which, insofar as they coincide with those of the author, the interpreter must assume to be present until the opposite be proven, if the interpretation is not to be unfair to the author. We will not always be able to dismiss the consequences implicit in this postulate with the shoulder-shrugging smile Meier draws from us when he demands in the interest of hermeneutic fairness that in interpretation the virtuous meanings be given preference to the vicious, the pious to the impious, the chaste to the unchaste. The question alone of whether usage, convention, is a hermeneutic principle and if so, whether it is sufficient or insufficient is among the problems of hermeneutics that are still relevant. Chladenius proceeds from the notion that one "can learn the common [i.e., nonmetaphorical] meaning of words from their use in different circumstances" (p. 281). Meier sees in this correspondence with usage one of the perfections of artificial, or arbitrary, signs.

He who uses arbitrary signs [...] should [...] always imitate natural signs in signifying things insofar as it is possible to do so. Thus the arbitrary signs he uses, and which were invented by others, should be as intelligible and clear as possible. This indisputable intelligibility can be maintained if he associates with the sign that meaning which most people who use the sign usually associate with it. And thus evolves the *customary signification (usus signandi)*, or the agreement among those who use certain signs to associate certain meanings with them. In interpreting arbitrary signs, therefore, an interpreter must assume the meaning which accords with the customary signification to be true, until the opposite be proven. (§97, pp. 51f.)

This notion, which ought really to be evaluated in connection with what Friedrich Schlegel called the "postulate of the common" in the twenty-fifth *Lyceum* fragment,[5] implies a hierarchy of different *sensus* in interpretation. Because the proper [or literal] meaning of words tends to be more familiar and more frequent than the improper meaning and thus tends to occur more frequently to those who use the words, the former, the proper meaning, is clearer than the latter, the metaphorical meaning,

because the latter cannot be known from words without wit and the kind of comparison with the proper meaning that wit effects. An interpreter will therefore always prefer the proper, straightforward meaning to the improper, until the opposite becomes evident. Therefore, in interpretation one should not deviate unnecessarily from the proper meaning of the words, all the less so the more imperfect and far-fetched the improper, figurative, and allegorical, etc., meaning is. (§172, pp. 91f.)

It would be easy to expose the historical element in this thesis – the Enlightenment's criticism of Scholastic allegoresis and Baroque allegory. But the fact of such devaluing of metaphorical expression over against nonmetaphorical expression is less important to hermeneutics than the question of whether what Meier set in motion with his postulate of hermeneutic fairness does not live on in our own interpretive practice, which rejects this kind of hierarchy – with a different justification, but without accounting for this preference and the reasons for it.

Thus I would like to conclude the presentation of Meier's art of interpretation, and along with it the part of our study dedicated to the period of the Enlightenment, with a programmatic observation. It ought to be the task of contemporary hermeneutics to ask of contemporary interpretive practice among other things whether in inquiring into the meaning of a passage it employs the working hypothesis that the passage is metaphorical, or nonmetaphorical, in

[5] "The two basic maxims of the so-called historical criticism are the postulate of the common and the axiom of the ordinary. Postulate of the common: Everything really great, good, and beautiful, is improbable, since it is extraordinary and therefore at least suspect. Axiom of the ordinary: Our conditions and environment must have existed everywhere, for they are really so natural." Friedrich Schlegel, *Dialogue on Poetry and Literary Aphorisms*, tr., ed., and intro. Ernst Behler and Roman Struc (University Park, 1968), p. 123.

nature. If this is the case, it would be necessary to ask further about the criteria underlying such a working hypothesis. I will mention a few possibilities: the notion that the nonmetaphorical use as the "proper," over against the "improper," is also the obvious one, so that the metaphorical use must prove itself (i.e., the working hypothesis that the passage is not a metaphor must be falsified). Or the provisional anticipatory decision, as the working hypothesis may be characterized, is guided by the genre to which the work belongs. Or the working hypothesis turns out not to be disinterested – for the more metaphorical the text, the richer the haul for interpretation, as is well known. Or, on the other hand, as a final speculation, the working hypothesis appears as an expectation that is always dependent on the context, whether as counterdetermination, which Harald Weinrich considers a characteristic of metaphor,[6] or as analogy, which suspects a word of being a metaphor because a word that stands in its context and corresponds to it has already been construed as a metaphor. Certainly such an analysis of hermeneutic practice will have to turn into a critique thereof (in the Königsberg, not the Dahlem sense):[7] into questioning the premises of those prior decisions that we always make whenever we interpret a text, and to recognizing the conditional nature of our activities – from both of which we are least liberated when we ignore them.

[6] See Harald Weinrich, *Tempus. Besprochene und erzählte Welt* (Stuttgart, 1964), p. 108.
[7] An allusion to the "Critical University" established within the Free University of Berlin during the 1960s. A creation of the then radical, largely Marxist student union there, it sponsored an alternative curriculum which attracted large numbers of students away from official University courses, catalyzing the kind of curricular change to which Szondi alludes on p. 68 above.

8

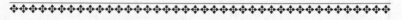

Ast

At least from the time of Dilthey's 1900 essay on "The Development of Hermeneutics," Schleiermacher's has been the first name to occur to anyone speaking or hearing of hermeneutics in Germany. When Dilthey celebrates him as the founder of a scientific hermeneutics, it is not merely on account of the high position Schleiermacher held among his contemporaries, nor because of the intensity with which he worked on the problems of hermeneutics in the two-and-a-half decades between 1805 and 1829. (His earliest notes on the subject date from 1805 and he delivered his two addresses on the concept of hermeneutics in 1829 in Berlin.) Dilthey's essay also bears witness to the affinity between the methodology he himself framed for the humanities and Schleiermacher's hermeneutics, an affinity which prevented Dilthey from doing justice to, say, the hermeneutics of the Enlightenment.[1] Without wishing to belittle Schleiermacher's contribution in the least, it is nevertheless impossible, upon examination of the historical premises and the contemporary state of hermeneutics, for us to follow Dilthey in viewing Schleiermacher as the founder of a new science, or discipline. We intend rather to place his concept of hermeneutics in historical context and to examine his theses on hermeneutics in terms of our contemporary understanding of literature and history.

The date of Schleiermacher's two addresses to the Academy, 1829, indicates that German Idealism arrived at its formulation of hermeneutics only very late. For from the point of view of the history of ideas, nothing new begins with Schleiermacher: his outline of hermeneutics is saturated rather with the insights and experiences of the preceding decades. Dilthey mentions "Winckelmann's interpretation of works of art," Herder's "congenial empathy with the spirit of ages and peoples, and the philological work done according to the

---

[1] Dilthey, "The Development of Hermeneutics," p. 254f.

new aesthetic perspective by Heyne, Friedrich August Wolf, and his disciples," but above all "the procedure of German transcendental philosophy of going beyond what is given to consciousness to a creative capacity which works in a unifying way, unconscious of itself, to generate the whole form of the world in us."[2] Thus Dilthey, whose interpretation of Kant as an existential philosopher is problematic enough. That the hermeneutics of that era is finally formulated so late, shortly before the end of the era and well after the formulation of its aesthetic, philosophical, and historiographical views, may be explained by the reflexive nature of this discipline. If knowledge, in Hegel's words,[3] is an activity of twilight, of the owl's flight, how much more so is knowledge about knowledge. But this means that Schleiermacher's hermeneutics can be understood only against the background of the intellectual landscape evoked by the names of Winckelmann and Herder, Kant and Fichte, Goethe and Schiller, Schelling and Hegel. Thus, in turning to Schleiermacher and his immediate predecessors after discussing the hermeneutic systems of Chladenius and Georg Friedrich Meier, we cannot really speak either of continuity or discontinuity. There is no real continuity because the half century that lies between Meier and Schleiermacher represents one of the most pronounced caesuras in intellectual history; there is no real discontinuity because a new, fully conceptualized hermeneutics first emerges only in the years after 1805, however much a new form of understanding may have been realized in the aesthetic, philosophical, and literary writings we have mentioned.

The two treatises that Schleiermacher presented in August and October 1829 to the plenary assembly of the Prussian Academy of Sciences are entitled *Ueber den Begriff der Hermeneutik, mit Bezug auf F. A. Wolfs Andeutungen und Asts Lehrbuch* [*On the Concept of Hermeneutics, with Reference to F. A. Wolf's Suggestions and Ast's Textbook*].[a] Schleiermacher thus did not view his outline of hermeneutics as a

[2] Ibid., p. 256.

[3] Georg Wilhelm Friedrich Hegel, "Preface," in *Hegel's Philosophy of Right*, tr. and ed. T. M. Knox (Oxford, 1942), p. 13.

[a] Collected in Friedrich Daniel Ernst Schleiermacher, *Hermeneutics: The Handwritten Manuscripts*, ed. and intro. Heinz Kimmerle, tr. James Duke and Jack Forstman (Missoula, 1977), pp. 175–214. This is a translation of Schleiermacher, *Hermeneutik*, new edn. on the basis of the manuscripts, ed. and intro. Heinz Kimmerle (Heidelberg, 1959), pp. 123–56. Subsequent references are to this translation; I have emended it where appropriate in the interest of a more literal rendering of the German.

creatio ex nihilo. Nor are the two classical philologists treated as representatives of a hermeneutics which must be overcome. Rather, Schleiermacher calls their works "the most significant to have appeared in this area" and continues:

As Wolf represents the finest mind, the freest genius among us, and Ast strives everywhere to proceed as a philosophically synthesizing philologist, it should be all the more instructive and beneficial to combine the two. Thus it seemed to me to be most expedient for now, since I am following these leaders, to join my own thoughts about the task [of hermeneutics] to their propositions. (pp. 176–77)

Schleiermacher's reference to his two predecessors, but also the fact that presentation of his hermeneutics runs into considerable difficulties on account of the number and variety of sources (notes from 1805–1809, the compendium of 1819, the Academy addresses of 1829, the notes taken on his lectures), make it reasonable to turn first to the section devoted to hermeneutics in one of the works he cites in the title of his Academy addresses: the 1808 *Grundlinien der Grammatik, Hermeneutik und Kritik* [*Outline of Grammar, Hermeneutics, and Criticism*] by Friedrich Ast, a professor of philology (i.e., classical philology) at the University of Landshut.[4] The hermeneutics of his far more famous colleague, the Homeric scholar Wolf, was not published until 1831, in the posthumous collection *Vorlesungen über die Alterthumswissenschaft* [*Lectures on Classical Studies*].[5] Wolf's "Suggestions" on hermeneutics, which Schleiermacher mentions along with Ast's textbook, appears in his "Darstellung der Alterthums-Wissenschaft" ["Presentation of Classical Studies"],[6] the opening piece in the first volume (1807) of the periodical *Museum der Alterthums-Wissenschaft*, which Wolf helped to edit. The volume is dedicated to Goethe, and the dedication makes it clear that it is not just in retrospect that the epoch appears as the Age of Goethe, that it also understood itself in these terms – at least insofar as its classicism is

[4] Friedrich Ast, *Grundlinien der Grammatik, Hermeneutik und Kritik* (Landshut, 1808), pp. 165–214. Subsequent references are given in the text.
[5] Friedrich August Wolf, "Vorlesung über die Encyclopädie der Alterthumswissenschaft," in Wolf, *Vorlesungen über die Alterthumswissenschaft*, vol. 1, ed. J. D. Gürtler (Leipzig, 1831), pp. 271–302.
[6] Friedrich August Wolf, "Darstellung der Alterthums-Wissenschaft," in *Museum der Alterthums-Wissenschaft*, vol. 1, ed. Friedrich August Wolf and Philipp Buttmann (Berlin, 1807), pp. 1–142. Also in Wolf, *Kleine Schriften in lateinischer und deutscher Sprache*, vol. 2 (Halle, 1869), pp. 803–95.

concerned. (The self-image of early Romanticism was no less shaped by Goethe, although through a kind of love-hatred.) The beginning of this dedication is the best introduction to the intellectual world whose first hermeneutic system is Ast's *Grundlinien*. It reads:

May Goethe, the connoisseur and exemplar of the Greek spirit, be pleased by this initial volume, presented with love, of a collection of writings and essays designed to enlighten here and there the spacious house of knowledge in which that life-enhancing spirit originally lived. – Who among the Germans would sooner come to mind, in an undertaking of this kind, than Goethe, in whose works and sketches that beneficent spirit has found a second home in the midst of horrifying modern surroundings?[7]

Only one word is repeated in these well-considered and ceremonious lines: three times the "Greek spirit" is invoked in them, "that life-enhancing, that beneficent spirit." This is the key to Ast's hermeneutics and the word that differentiates the "new" hermeneutics from that of the Enlightenment. All the differences between the hermeneutic notions of the mid-eighteenth century and those of the early nineteenth century can be derived from the introduction into hermeneutics of this concept, whose multivalent content and function make it difficult to grasp – a concept which would be unthinkable in the terminology of Enlightenment theories of interpretation. There it was a question of the meaning and application of a passage, of the intention of the author and of the thing signified by him – of rational matters, of the psychology of effects, of real things. In the hermeneutics of the Age of Goethe it is a question of spirit, of that spirit of Greece intuited in the wake of Winckelmann and Herder and of its enhancing and beneficent influence in a "horrifying modern" world, of an idealistic synthesis of aesthetics and ethics, in a form unknown to the Enlightenment, a synthesis which answers to the name of *humanism* and was in no small measure responsible for the ever-increasing alienation of the ideas of the leading intellects from political reality, which still held the attention of the authors of the Enlightenment – an alienation that finally led to barbarism.

Our discussion of Ast's *Grundlinien* will have to show the extent to which the concept of spirit not only serves to define the goal that hermeneutics in the Age of Goethe sets for understanding, but simultaneously sublates in its foggy aura all of the problems raised by, say, the temporal distance between author and reader or the

---

[7] *Museum der Alterthums-Wissenschaft*, pp. iii–iv.

interdependence of text and context. The hermeneutic thought of the Enlightenment either did not perceive these problems or ignored them because of its prejudice in favor of the ostensibly rational – by insisting, say, on authorial intention or by reducing the meaning of a passage to its subject matter.

It would be a great mistake, however, to reproach Ast merely for talking of spirit. He is to be faulted only for making it too easy for himself with such talk, for thinking that he could eliminate all questions and contradictions by invoking spirit instead of bringing the problems of hermeneutics before the court of philosophy, instead of weighing philological questions in terms of their philosophical implications and setting different expectations for their solution. He is to be faulted for granting spirit a harmonizing function. This distinction is important because with the ascendancy of Positivism, the philology of the Age of Goethe, as represented by Ast, fell into disrepute. That a philologist today can view that period as a scientific step backwards lasting over 150 years is an expression of idiosyncratic bias against the philological program which Ast put forward 160 years ago. According to his program, the philologist should

be not only a *master of languages* or an *antiquarian*, but also a *philosopher* and an *aesthetician*; he should be able not only to analyze the letter [*Buchstaben*] given him into its component parts but also to explore the spirit that shaped the letter so as to penetrate the higher meaning of the letter; and he should know how to appreciate the form in which the letter has presented itself for the revelation of the spirit. (p. iv)

Without this higher scientific life, Ast's "Foreword" continues, "philology is either mere *formalism* or mere *materialism* – the former regarded as one-sided linguistic research, the latter, as mere antiquarian learnedness" (p. iv). Nearly every word of this program could be subscribed to today – if it is a matter of freeing philosophy from the century-and-a-half of self-induced blindness in which it has posed as Justice itself, Justice in a blindfold, while merely becoming self-righteous. Well, not quite every word. For even, or rather especially, a philosophically informed philology must refuse to view everything that has to do with spirit as automatically higher than the letter. Such a philology especially will have always to ask itself unmercifully whether any spirit is expressed in the letter and if so, which spirit, instead of always declaring the letter the revelation of *the* spirit. And especially an aesthetically informed philology (that is, an aesthetics that proceeds according to philological methods) will have to be cautious about accepting Ast's thesis that "the *ultimate* thing that joins content and form into a living unity, hovering over both, dominating both, [is] *spirit*, the eternal formative principle of all life" (p. v; first emphasis Szondi's). For the task of this kind of philology has to be to analyze the relation of form and content in a given work instead of overhastily postulating a "living unity" and allowing the interpretation to be determined by this ideal vision. And with regard to "living unity" itself, we have to ask whether the concept is closer to Schelling's or to Hegel's and Hölderlin's. Must it be free of internal contradiction, as Schelling would have it? Can it appear to be harmonious only because unity is thought to be prior to empirical reality, or does it come into being as a product of oppositions in the real world, as a mediation between them, as in Hegel's dialectics and Hölderlin's poetics? But Ast was a student of Schelling's.

Ast perceives in spirit not only the condition of the possibility of understanding but also its goal. "All understanding and grasping not only of an alien world but of any other at all is absolutely impossible without the original unity and equality of everything spiritual and without the original unity of all things in spirit" (§70, pp. 167f.) For spirit, according to Ast, there is in essence absolutely nothing alien because spirit is the higher, infinite unity, the center of all life unbounded by any periphery. Whatever that may mean, for hermeneutics the question as to the characteristics and capabilities of this highest authority arises only insofar as the act of understanding is also placed under its aegis. And in fact this occurs in a polemical turn against seventeenth- and eighteenth-century Sensationalism. Ast writes:

That things enter the spirit from without, through images that flow in, through sense impressions, or whatever other non-explanatory explanations people have thought up, is a self-destroying and long since abandoned idea; being cannot change itself into spirit without being related to it or originally being one with it. (§69, pp. 166f.)

The sensationalism that is rejected here is the prerequisite of a hermeneutics oriented to subject matter such as we encountered in Chladenius and even in Meier. Interpretation there means understanding a passage which in turn is taken to be an explanation of a state of affairs. The author formulates his insight into the matter. The reader or interpreter understands the passage correctly when he recapitulates the author's insight into the matter, when he achieves the same insight into it. The problem of how an alien spirit can be understood at all does not arise for Enlightenment hermeneutics because it does not view understanding as understanding of the author but as understanding of his understanding. The unproblematized presupposition of such a view is the possibility of understanding the things of this world – a possibility which even in Meier is based on the semiotic character of things, on the adaption of creation to interpretation by man – *explicatio naturae*. The turning point in the history of hermeneutics occurs when in Ast and in Schleiermacher the object of understanding ceases to be the passage or text – which in their turn refer to a subject matter knowledge of which is represented therein and constitutes the final goal of interpretation – and becomes instead the author. Strictly speaking, it is here that understanding first appears as a hermeneutic act, displacing exegesis. The orderly course that Dilthey observed in the history of hermeneutics, leading from unregulated philological practice to the formulation of rules and from there to systematization of the rules and finally to the analysis of understanding, which is to be "the secure basis for the formulation of rules,"[8] proves to be most problematic from this perspective. Basing hermeneutics on the analysis of understanding is not after all simply a sign of progress in the development of hermeneutics but also the result of a change in the object of interpretation, a change which in its turn can be traced to the turn in epistemology from Sensationalism to Criticism and Idealism.

It is relevant to the above-mentioned critique of the harmonizing function of spirit as Ast conceives it that spirit, as that which makes understanding possible (since all things are originally one in spirit and everything spiritual is originally one and the same), also guarantees a solution to all hermeneutic problems – those posed by factual differences, by two different meanings of the same word, by the temporal distance between author and reader, by the difference in the interpretive movements from the whole to the part and from the part to the whole, which reciprocally presuppose one another, thus creating the problem of the hermeneutic circle. All of these problems are solved from the outset by the concept of spirit – at the cost, of course, that the solution is secured in theory only, and that because it does not involve the formulation of rules, it misses the road to praxis. In this respect recourse to the process of understanding, at least in

---

[8] Dilthey, "The Development of Hermeneutics," p. 249.

Ast's work, is precisely not what Dilthey claims it to be: a "secure basis for the formulation of rules"[9] – and we will have to ask later whether this changes in the works of Schleiermacher and Dilthey.[10]

The following passage should clarify how Ast's concept of spirit, rather than furnishing a solution, performs a disappearing act on the problem of temporal distance, which becomes acute for hermeneutics with the rise of historical consciousness in the second half of the eighteenth century (Herder):

> [We could] understand neither antiquity in general nor a work of art nor a text if our spirit were not essentially and originally one with the spirit of antiquity, so that it is able to assume the other, only temporally and relatively alien, spirit into itself. For it is only temporal and external factors (upbringing, education, situation, etc.) that create a difference of spirit; if one abstracts from the temporal and external, as accidental differences relative to pure spirit, then all spirit is the same. And this is precisely the goal of *philological* education: to purify spirit of the temporal, accidental, and subjective and to impart to it the originality and versatility, in a word, the *humanism* that is necessary to the higher, pure man to the end that he may grasp the true, the good, and the beautiful in all forms and representations, however alien, transforming them into his own being, and thus again become one with the original, purely human spirit from which he has been separated by the limitations of his time, his education, and his situation.   (§70, pp. 168f.)

Here, no less than in Ast's sketch of the philosophy of history, which we will discuss shortly, the influence of Schelling is clear. As in Schelling, all differences are reduced to relative differences, what appears different is essentially identical, with the result that the task of cognition lies in purging the temporal, the external, and the accidental. Just as it is beyond doubt that understanding the spirit of antiquity – to retain that expression for the moment – is possible only on the basis of the identity of the spiritual, it must be stressed that this is no absolute identity, that the spirit of antiquity is no longer that of antiquity once it is freed of its strangeness. To be sure, understanding an alien spirit depends on an affinity, a sense that it is not absolutely alien, but the object is the alien spirit precisely *qua* alien, so understanding must not occur through the reduction of the alien element to a constant – this would simply be a mirror of the understanding subject.

---

[9] Ibid, p. 250.
[10] Szondi had intended to treat Dilthey in the second part of the course, which was not given. See the translator's preface, p. xxvi, above.

In considering Ast's conception of the historicity of works and of the dismantling of this historicity in understanding, we must not ignore the fact that his hermeneutics has as its object only the understanding of works of antiquity. The Enlightenment attempts of, say, Chladenius and Meier, to establish a general theory of interpretation are followed by a return to specialized hermeneutics, from which Schleiermacher will be the first to turn away. It is, of course, peculiar that Ast does not consider an explanation of this limitation or a survey of other hermeneutic systems neccessary: his *Grundlinien der Grammatik, Hermeneutik und Kritik*, which was originally to be an appendix to his *Grundriss der Philologie* [*Outline of Philology*], which also appeared in 1808, treats as equally a matter of course only the questions that arise in dealing with texts from Greek and Roman antiquity – as "philology" at this time meant only "classical philology."

It is thus that the task which Ast assigns to "philological education" (p. 169) – namely, the purging of spirit of the temporal, the accidental, and the subjective – could appear as a classicism that rose above all historical givens and had no doubts about the relevance (and hence also the suitability for imitation) of the art and poetry of antiquity. But retention of the historical physiognomy of Greek art is absolutely necessary to the imitative classicism of Winckelmann, and imitation can become a postulate for him only because Winckelmann considers the historical givens of his time ill-disposed to art – so that the idea is not so much to take off an historical costume as to change costumes (or more precisely, since we do not experience our own clothes as a costume, to put on a costume). Classicism as represented by Ast, on the other hand, has been embedded in a conception of the philosophy of history. This conception coincides in decisive points with Schelling's as presented in his *Philosophie der Kunst* [*Philosophy of Art*]. Ast was Schelling's student in Jena, and in 1805 he propagated Schelling's unpublished aesthetics, the lectures given in Jena in 1802–03, in his *System der Kunstlehre* [*System of Aesthetics*].

Following the passage cited above about man's reunion with the "original, purely human spirit, from which he has been separated by the limitations of his time, his education, and his situation" (p. 169), we read that this is

not merely an idea, as it might appear to those who oppose the actual, as the only reality and sole truth, to the ideal (p. 169); for the higher type of history (not the kind that merely assembles facts) proves this conclusively. Just as

mankind is essentially one, it was one also temporally, in the most glorious
plenitude and purity of its life forces: in the oriental world, which is only
mythical and religious because it did not yet know the temporal opposition
between real and ideal education. For paganism and Christianity are, for
instance, still one in the Indian world: God is both plenitude or all (pantheism)
and the unity of all life (theism) at once. Only after the dissolution of
Orientalism did its individual characteristics emerge in time (as periods in the
education of mankind). This is where history in the strict sense begins – the
life of mankind unfolding successively over time. The two poles of history are
the Greek and the Christian worlds, both of which, however, emerged from
one central point, Orientalism, and by virtue of their original unity strive for
reunion in our world. The triumph of *our* education will therefore be the free,
consciously created harmony of the poetic (plastic or Greek) and the religious
(musical or Christian) life of the education of man.   (§70, pp. 170f.)

Ast adds in conclusion:

Thus everything proceeds from one spirit and strives back toward one spirit.
Without the recognition of this original unity, which flees itself (divides itself
temporally) and seeks itself again, we are incapable not only of understanding
antiquity, but also of knowing anything at all about history and the education
of man.   (§70, p. 171)

The precondition for Ast's hermeneutics is thus not an ahistorical
imitative classicism. Instead, the hermeneutic process, the understanding of antiquity, becomes itself an historical act – indeed, not
simply an historically conditioned act, but an act which creates history.
It becomes a moment in the development of the spirit which is striving
toward unity with itself from the temporal opposition in which it had
manifested itself – Hellenism and Christianity. Understanding col-
laborates in this return of spirit to itself, by joining together antiquity,
which lives on in the works to be understood, and Christianity, to
which the understanding subject belongs. This synthesis of the Greek
and Christian, which the late poetry of Hölderlin, for instance, also
aspires to at about the same time, could even be called *the* task of
hermeneutics.

Ast's treatment of the problem of temporal distance in hermeneutics
shows that he no longer believes it can be eliminated merely by
replacing a sign that has aged, as the adherents of grammatical
interpretation believed. But since he views spirit as essentially
unhistorical and the temporal as merely relative, and builds the
relationship of the modern reader to the ancient text into the
movement of the spirit in its return to itself, the question as to how
historical knowledge is possible becomes irrelevant. What Dilthey will

later call the critique of historical reason[11] has become superfluous in Ast thanks to the premises of Identity philosophy and the philosophy of history.

The concept of spirit serves the same function in his treatment of the hermeneutic circle.

The basic law of all understanding and knowing is to find the spirit of the whole from the part and through the whole to grasp the part; the former is the analytical, the latter the synthetic, method of knowing. But both are possible only with and through each other, just as the whole cannot be thought without the part, as its element, and the part cannot be thought without the whole, as the sphere in which it exists. Neither is prior to the other because both are mutually dependent and form essentially one harmonious life. Thus the spirit of antiquity as a whole cannot be truly apprehended unless we grasp it in its individual manifestations, the works of its writers; and conversely, the spirit of a writer cannot be comprehended without the spirit of the whole of antiquity.

But if we can apprehend the spirit of antiquity as a whole only through its manifestation in the works of its writers, and yet we need knowledge of the universal spirit to understand them, then how is it possible, since we can only comprehend one thing after another and not the whole all at once, to know the individual work, since this presupposes knowledge of the whole? We cannot break the circle within which I can comprehend a, b, c, etc. only after I know A, but knowledge of this A in turn depends on knowing a, b, c, as long as we regard A and a, b, c as oppositions which are mutually dependent and presuppose each other. But we can break the circle if we recognize their unity, if we recognize that A does not simply proceed from, is not simply constituted by a, b, c, etc., but instead precedes them and permeates all of them in the same way, such that a, b, c are nothing other than individual representations of the one A. In A are already contained, in an original way, a, b, and c; these elements are themselves the individual manifestations of the one A, so that in each of them A is already contained in a particular way; and I need not go through the whole infinite series of details in order to find their unity.

This is the only way in which it is possible to comprehend the part through the whole and conversely the whole through the part; for both are simultaneously given in every detail; A is given along with a because the latter is only a manifestation of A; the whole, in short, is given along with every part; and the further I progress in grasping the part, going through the series a, b, c, etc., the more obvious and vital the spirit becomes to me, the more the idea of the whole unfolds which emerged for me with the first element of the series. Spirit is never an accretion of details; it is always an

---

[11] See Wilhelm Dilthey, *Gesammelte Schriften*, vol. 7, 4th edn. (Stuttgart and Göttingen, 1964), pp. 191ff.

Chapter 8

original, simple, undivided essence. In each detail, therefore, it is just as simple, whole, and undivided as it is in itself; that is, every detail is simply the particular, phenomenal form of the one spirit. The part thus does not generate the spirit or the idea, create it by accretion, but stimulates it, awakens it.

(§75, pp. 178ff.)

If we recall Heidegger's dictum that "what is decisive is not to get out of the circle, but to come into it in the right way,"[12] the first thing to bear in mind is that for Ast the hermeneutic circle is still a logical and methodological scandal: the circle *must* be broken. He claims that the circle will remain unbreakable as long as both elements, the part (or more precisely, the series of details) and the whole, are thought of as opposites. But to this it must be objected that the demand that the circle be broken, the characterization of it as breakable/unbreakable, presupposes thinking in oppositions. It does not follow from thinking of the part and the whole as opposites that the circle is unbreakable, but only that the circle is being judged according to the law of noncontradiction and thus is found to be unbreakable.

What Ast presents as a solution to the problem of the hermeneutic circle is therefore closer to its negation. Instead of an interdependence of analytic and synthetic methods, of cognition based on the part and cognition based on the whole – an interdependence which, if it is not experienced as a logical contradiction, indicates that understanding is a process and as such is essentially open-ended – we find in Ast the a priori identity of part and whole. The details are enfolded in the whole, the whole lies in specific form in the part. Because the telos of understanding for Ast is the spirit, the part alone becomes, to use Meier's term, the hermeneutic ground. Analytic and synthetic methods are not viewed as interdependent and employed alternately in the circular movement of understanding. Instead, understanding proceeds purely analytically, starting with the part but certain that this part is also always the whole. Analysis is simultaneously synthesis. In contrast to the way in which we conceive of the hermeneutic circle today, the whole, *qua* spirit, is too good to serve as the hermeneutic ground and to illuminate the part in turn as the part sheds light on the whole. The "whole" – which, unless fixed by Identity philosophy, is constantly changing insofar as it is the momentary configuration of all of the details grasped up to that point – is relieved of this hermeneutic function in Ast's system. Consequently, comprehension of a detail –

[12] Heidegger, *Being and Time*, p. 195.

105

concretely, of an author of antiquity – cannot orient itself by reference to what, on the basis of comparison, several authors of the period appear to have in common. (The idea of what they have in common presupposes in turn the understanding of the individual authors that orients itself by reference to that idea – here we have the hermeneutic circle.) The postulate is rather that the very first detail stimulates the idea of the whole because the spirit, as original, undivided essence, must also be whole and undivided in each part. In concrete terms, the sprit of an age must be present in this way in every individual author. Because the particular, following Schelling, is admitted only as something apparent behind which the spirit as the universal asserts itself in its self-identity, understanding the part is no longer dependent on understanding the whole. The postulate of the whole as present in the part, of the universal as present in the particular, is thus the presupposition for what Ast presents as the breaking of the hermeneutic circle. Just as his philosophy of history renders the question as to the possibility of historical knowledge superfluous, so too do the premises he adopts from Identity philosophy obviate the question as to the possibility of understanding under the conditions imposed by the hermeneutic circle.

Ast does not view the interpretation of individual textual passages as a hermeneutic act, let alone restrict interpretation to specific passages, the obscure ones, as was the case with Chladenius. As a result, "understanding a work" can no longer mean for him understanding all the passages of the work. Since he postulates that the idea of the whole is awakened in the understanding subject by the first detail understood – because the spirit of the whole already resides in each individual element – the process of understanding and interpretation loses the additive character it had had throughout the entire tradition of hermeneutics. Understanding becomes an unfolding in which the idea of the whole (contained in every detail and thus intuitable from the very first detail grasped) becomes concrete as the work is processed in the succession of individual acts of understanding. This means that the act of understanding, as a genetic act, recapitulates the genesis of literature. "The understanding and explanation of a work [is] a true re-creation [*Nachbilden*] of a creation [*des schon Gebildeten*]" (§80, p. 187). The significance of this thesis for the history of hermeneutics can hardly be overestimated – it marks its most decisive turning point. We will treat this thoroughly in our discussion of Schleiermacher; let us merely note here that Ast conceives of the

genesis of the individual literary work on the model of the evolution
of the spirit as – borrowing from Schelling – specified by his philosophy of history. And just as this Idealist conception makes all of the
questions relevant to a critique of historical reason seem to be always
already answered, defining the genetic process likewise answers in
advance all of the questions that a genetic mode of interpretation
would pose with regard to a specific work. This is demonstrated by the
example Ast adduces to clarify his characterization of understanding
as a re-creation of a creation.

In an Horatian ode [...] explanation will start at the very point at which the
poet's production began; the idea of the whole is intimated therein just as
certainly as the starting point of the poetic production itself originated in the
inspired idea of the whole. The idea of the whole unfolds, after it has received
its initial direction in its starting point, pervading all elements of the poem;
and the explanation has to grasp these individual moments, each in its own
individual life, until the circle of evolving elements is full, the totality of
details flows back into the idea with which the production began, the
manifold life realized in the details becomes one again with the original unity
that was only intimated in the first represented moment of the production;
and the unity that was initially still indeterminate becomes a visible, living
harmony.   (§81, pp. 189f.)

No doubt it *could* be like this. But whether or not it is in a given case
– whether the starting point of literary production already indicates
the idea of the whole, whether this idea pervades all of the elements
of the work or whether there are also some that do not relate to the
idea of the whole, whether, further, the individual parts of the work
unite harmoniously or not, and finally whether the totality of details
flows back into the idea with which the production began or possibly
transcends the starting point instead – this seems to me exactly what
needs to be tested in genetic interpretation, in a reconstruction of the
history of a work's genesis. Instead, the genesis to be investigated is
here assumed in advance (necessarily) to coincide with the unfolding
of spirit as defined by Identity philosophy.

    Since re-production of a work's genesis replaces the interpretation
of textual passages in Ast's system, the doctrine of manifold textual
meanings, as it was developed in patristic and Scholastic hermeneutics
from their beginnings in Greece and Alexandria and was still alive in
the Enlightenment, loses its justification. The distinction between the
sensus litteralis and the *sensus spiritualis*, a distinction in the subject
matter, is replaced by a distinction between ways of regarding and

interpreting. It is no longer the meaning that is multiple, but understanding. Thus Ast distinguishes between *historical* understanding, which relates to content, *grammatical* understanding, which relates to form, language, and style, and *spiritual* understanding, which focuses on the spirit of the individual writer and the epoch. Presentation of the most essential features of Schleiermacher's hermeneutics will reveal how this reform, brought about by the displacement of the hermeneutics of the individual passage, affected the theory of interpretation.

Schleiermacher, I

In turning to Schleiermacher's hermeneutics, which underwent a number of modifications during a span of nearly three decades, from 1805 to 1833, let us employ some of the insights gained in our discussion of Ast, and by focusing on the areas in which he diverges from eighteenth-century hermeneutics, attempt to ascertain what Ast's and Schleiermacher's hermeneutic systems have in common and how they differ. The fact that Ast's system is shaped by the Identity philosophy of Schelling explains why his name was long forgotten in the history of hermeneutics while Schleiermacher, at least since Dilthey, has been considered the most important representative, even the founder, of philosophical hermeneutics. If this is an explanation, then it is not simply because Ast's theses stand or fall with the validity of Schelling's Identity philosophy, but because these philosophical premises do not so much formulate, or solve, the problems of hermeneutics as make them appear to have been already solved. Schleiermacher, by contrast, displays an extremely keen awareness of problems, as may be seen in the numerous modifications of his hermeneutic theory over the years.

Of course, the history of the development of Schleiermacher's hermeneutics has only recently become an object of scholarly investigation. Dilthey's image of Schleiermacher, and hence the image for the first six decades of our century (because Dilthey's authority on this matter was hardly questioned until 1959), is based on the hermeneutic texts contained in the edition of his *Sämmtliche Werke [Complete Works]*[1] begun in the year of his death, 1834: the two Academy addresses of 1829 and *Hermeneutik und Kritik [Hermeneutics and Criticism]*,[2] edited

---

[1] Friedrich Daniel Ernst Schleiermacher, *Sämmtliche Werke*, 31 vols. (Berlin, 1835–64).

[2] Friedrich Daniel Ernst Schleiermacher, *Hermeneutik und Kritik mit besonderer Beziehung auf das Neue Testament*, ed. Friedrich Lücke, in *Sämmtliche Werke*, pt. 1, vol. 7 (Berlin, 1838).

by Friedrich Lücke on the basis of Schleiermacher's literary estate and notes on his lectures. Only in 1959 did Heinz Kimmerle's new edition, inspired by Gadamer, appear in the Heidelberg Academy of Sciences series.[a] Unlike Lücke 120 years earlier, Kimmerle, a student of Gadamer's, did not aim to produce a more or less coherent work (the textual history is reminiscent of that of Hegel's *Ästhetik*), but rather to reproduce Schleiermacher's authentic texts as they existed in manuscript, however fragmentary and mutually contradictory they might be. This edition begins with the aphorisms of 1805 and 1809 and closes with marginalia from 1832–33; in between there is a first draft from the period between 1810 and 1819, a compendium- or handbook-like presentation from 1819, the separate treatment of the second part of the compendium from the period between 1820 and 1829, and finally the Academy addresses of 1829. Only since the appearance of this edition has it been possible to trace the development of Schleiermacher's hermeneutics and examine its reception and interpretation by Dilthey. That was also the express aim of Kimmerle, who received his doctorate in 1957 with a dissertation entitled "Die Hermeneutik Schleiermachers im Zusammenhang seines spekulativen Denkens" ["Schleiermacher's Hermeneutics in the Context of His Speculative Thought"].[3] In the introduction to the edition he tried, in a few pages, to sketch out the history of this development in opposition to Dilthey's interpretation. (Kimmerle's presentation is heavily influenced by Gadamer's dispute with Dilthey and historicism.) In going back to the early stages of Schleiermacher's hermeneutics that were neglected by Lücke and even more so by Dilthey, Kimmerle emphasizes grammatical interpretation and the understanding of language which takes place therein instead of the kind of "psychological re-creation" in which the temporal distance between author and reader (in the sense specified by historicism) is annulled.[4]

In our discussion of Schleiermacher's hermeneutic ideas, we of course cannot interpret the various stages individually, but we must point out differences where they exist. Since we cannot present a developmental history, we shall take the most self-contained text, the two Academy addresses of 1829, as a starting point and will try to

---

[a] Schleiermacher, *Hermeneutik* (see p. 95, n. a above).

[3] Heinz Kimmerle, "Die Hermeneutik Schleiermachers im Zusammenhang seines spekulativen Denkens," dissertation (typewritten), Heidelberg, 1957.

[4] Heinz Kimmerle, "Editor's Introduction," in Schleiermacher, *Hermeneutics: The Handwritten Manuscripts*, pp. 27–28.

identify what is specific to their theses in relation to Friedrich Ast's on the one hand and to those of the earlier Schleiermacher on the other. We can summarize what was concluded about Ast in five points that distinguish him from the hermeneutics of the Enlightenment. While the problems contained in these five points may also be applicable to Schleiermacher, their solutions, or more precisely, the apparent solutions they owe to Identity philosophy, are not.

(1) The task of hermeneutic activity, which had previously consisted in explicating individual "obscure" passages, becomes that of understanding the author. The question as to how another person, a stranger, can be understood is unknown to Enlightenment hermeneutics, because it considers texts not as the expression of their authors but as the latter's explanation of a third thing, the object of the passage. Author and interpreter agree on this third thing. Ast solves the problem of understanding a stranger by postulating something common to everyone: the spirit.

(2) Ast also solves the problem of temporal distance by positing an eternally identical and ahistorical spirit. The temporal is relative and we must abstract from it in order to know the spirit. In addition to this, the historical distance of interpretation from the text is always the same for Ast because his hermeneutics applies only to the works of antiquity.

(3) The problem of the hermeneutic circle, unknown to Chladenius and Meier, likewise appears in Ast as always already solved. He does not see in the circle the precondition for understanding, but instead a contradiction which can be eliminated because the whole is posited as contained in the part. This does away with the interdependence between the analytic and synthetic methods: knowledge of the part is also always knowledge of the whole.

(4) Since understanding a text is no longer regarded as understanding the totality of its passages but as understanding the author and his relationship to the text, the genetic method replaces the additive method. Understanding, according to Ast, is re-creation of what has been created. The history of the work's genesis is not specific to each work for Ast but instead obeys a uniform law: the starting point of literary production lies in the idea of the whole, and this, after it has unfolded, or realized itself, in the sequence of individual moments, flows back into the starting point.

(5) Ast replaces the theory of manifold textual meaning with that of manifold modes of interpretation. He distinguishes historical under-

standing, which relates to content; grammatical understanding, which relates to form, language, and style; and spiritual understanding, which focuses on the spirit of the individual author and of the epoch.

We preface our discussion with these five points outlining Ast's position because in his Academy addresses Schleiermacher presents his thoughts, as his title states, "with reference to F. A. Wolf's suggestions and Ast's textbook."[5] But this does not mean that Schleiermacher first began to grapple with hermeneutic problems in response to Wolf and Ast. As previously noted, his earliest notes, as they date from 1805, were written *before* the appearance of Wolf's and Ast's works. In an autobiographical sketch, later discarded, which was to have prefaced his address, Schleiermacher makes reference to the reason for his interest in hermeneutic theory: in the context of his exegetical lectures on the New Testament it became clear to him that traditional theological hermeneutics consisted only in a collection of rules that "[lacked] a proper foundation because the general principles were nowhere established." Schleiermacher's hermeneutics is thus from the outset intended not as a continuation of traditional hermeneutics but as its theoretical foundation. He believes one of the reasons his immediate predecessors – the authors of hermeneutic works in use around 1800 (including neither Chladenius nor Meier) – did not come to such a theory of hermeneutics is that their works always related to only *one* kind of text: to the New Testament, as was the case with the 1761 *Institutio* of Johann August Ernesti, or to works of antiquity. Since these works of theological and philological hermeneutics take the specific problems of their subject matter as their starting point, they arrive only at rules designed to govern the interpretation of those particular writings or at most, like Ast, at a theory of the interpretaton of works of antiquity determined by the philosophy of history – but not at a theory of hermeneutics that could claim to be valid for all varieties of writing. Schleiermacher thus returns to the orientation of Enlightenment hermeneutics and the attempts to construct a general theory of interpretation to be found in Chladenius and Meier. But in contrast to them he does not seek the basis for a nonspecialized hermeneutics in the identical structure of

[5] Subsequent quotations deviate from the Kimmerle edition (see p. 95, n. a above) in that Schleiermacher's marginal notes are not identified as such.

textual passages, as Chladenius,[6] or in their semiotic character, as Meier,[7] but rather in the act of understanding, in interpretation itself.

By beginning with the fact of understanding in his effort to provide a foundation for hermeneutics, Schleiermacher does not merely abstract from the differences between works of antiquity and the Scriptures; he simultaneously extends the field of hermeneutics by making every linguistic object, as an object of understanding, the object of the theory of understanding, that is, of hermeneutics. Hermeneutics, he holds, is not concerned only with the works of writers, as Ast teaches, nor, as Wolf believes, only with works in a foreign language. Not only can texts other than literary texts, for example, newspapers and advertisements, present hermeneutic problems; spoken discourse, too, is a possible object of hermeneutics, one to which Schleiermacher even gives particular attention. In the first Academy address we read that

[...] hermeneutics is not to be limited to written texts. I often make use of hermeneutics in personal conversation when, discontented with the ordinary level of understanding, I wish to explore how my friend has moved from one thought to another or try to trace out the views, judgments, and aspirations which led him to speak about a given subject in just this way and no other. No doubt everyone has such experiences, and I think they make it clear that the task for which we seek a theory is not limited to what is fixed in writing but arises whenever we have to understand a thought or series of thoughts expressed in words. (pp. 181–2)

As revealing as this is, it must nevertheless be emphasized that in beginning with the act of understanding, Schleiermacher not only extends the field of hermeneutics but at the same time essentially modifies its task. For it is no longer simply a matter of comprehending the meaning of a given passage; we are supposed to understand its genesis: its connection with everything else and its motivation. Hermeneutics does not come into play for Schleiermacher where there are difficulties in understanding, but where "the ordinary level of understanding" does not seem sufficient. In the compendium-like presentation of 1819, he writes:

The art of interpretation is not equally interested in every act of speaking. Some instances fail to spark its interest at all, while others engage it completely. Most, however, fall somewhere between these two extremes. [...] An utterance may be regarded as being of no interest when it is neither important as a human act nor significant to the language. It occurs because the

---

[6] See Chapter 2, pp. 15ff. [7] See Chapter 6, pp. 68ff.

language maintains itself only by constant repetition. But that which is only already available and repeated is of no significance in itself. Conversations about the weather. These utterances are not absolutely devoid of significance, however, but rather may be said to be "minimally significant," in that they are constructed in the same way as more profound statements. (pp. 101–2)

This modification of the task of hermeneutics effects its emancipation from the disciplines as whose auxiliary it is usually regarded: theology, philology, jurisprudence. Schleiermacher says in the first Academy address:

I admit that I consider the practice of hermeneutics in one's native language and in intimate communication among people a very essential part of cultured life, apart from all philological or theological studies. Who could move in the company of exceptionally gifted people without endeavoring to hear "between" their words, just as we read between the lines of ingenious and densely written books? Who does not try in a significant conversation that could easily result in significant actions to lift out its vital points, to try to grasp its internal coherence, to pursue all its subtle intimations further?
(p. 182)

Schleiermacher does not stop at equating speech and writing as hermeneutic objects; to the interpreter of written works he says that he would

urgently recommend diligent practice in the interpretation of significant conversations. The immediate presence of the speaker, the living expression that proclaims that his whole being is involved, the way the thoughts in a conversation develop from our shared life, such factors stimulate us far more than some solitary observation of an isolated text to understand a series of thoughts as a moment of life which is breaking forth, as an act set in the context of many others. And this dimension of understanding is often slighted, in fact, almost completely neglected, in interpreting writers.
(p. 183)

These sentences reveal especially clearly the orientation of Schleier-macher's hermeneutics as well as the relevance he necessarily had for the existential philosophy of the late nineteenth century: it is not a matter of interpreting individual passages but of comprehending what is spoken and written in its origin in the individual life of its author: speech and writing viewed as a "moment of life breaking forth" and at the same time as an act, that is, not merely as a document but as an active, vital expression of life. It is obvious why this aspect, as Schleiermacher complains, was "almost completely neglected" in the hermeneutics of his time. As long as hermeneutics was specialized hermeneutics, the theory of the interpretation of the Holy Scriptures or the written monuments of antiquity, questions about the meaning of the text dominated the field because it was almost impossible to get behind the text to the totality of an author's (say, Homer's) life. Were we to inquire today into the justification of the hermeneutic orientation represented by Schleiermacher, we should have to turn our attention to the debate that has been going on for decades in literary studies over the tradition of existential philosophy and experiential psychology of the Dilthey school: in formalism, in New Criticism, in the "art of interpretation,"[b] in structuralism. Strangely enough, it is in France especially that Schleiermacher's decisive step from the written text back to speech, occasioned by his dissatisfaction with the "solitary observation of an isolated text," is at the center of discussion today – without Schleiermacher being named. I am thinking on the one hand of Georges Poulet's approach to literature, strongly influenced by Dilthey, which has recourse to the subjective (which is *not* to say the private) processes of perception and consciousness. On the other hand I am thinking of a literary theory, which probably derives from Mallarmé, the central concept of which is *écriture* and which is represented by, among others, Roland Barthes and Gérard Genette but especially Jacques Derrida.[8]

Schleiermacher found the most suggestive formulation for the contrast beween the older hermeneutics of the individual passage and his own hermeneutics as early as 1805, in one of his first aphorisms: "Two divergent maxims for understanding. (1) I understand everything until I encounter a contradiction or nonsense. (2) I do not understand anything that I do not perceive as necessary and cannot construe" (p. 41). Chladenius considers a contradiction to be a sign of the obscurity of a passage; his theory – like every traditional theory – of interpretation is activated whenever a passage is not immediately comprehensible, that is, when it appears to contradict the context or the presumed intention of the writer or acknowledged truth. Understanding is the resolution of the contradiction – a view whose rationalistic motivation is obvious. Schleiermacher represents the position of the second maxim according to which something is

---

[b] As disseminated by Emil Staiger. See p. 4, n. a above.

[8] See Roland Barthes, *Critique et vérité* (Paris, 1966); Gérard Genette, *Figures of Literary Discourse*, tr. Alan Sheridan, intro. Marie-Rose Logan (New York, 1982); Jacques Derrida, *Of Grammatology*, tr. Gayatri Chakravorty Spivak (Baltimore, 1976).

understood only when it is perceived as necessary and can be construed. Both criteria require a genetic view: the necessity of an expression is demonstrated when it can be derived from something else; understanding it thus presupposes recourse to the author, to the totality of his life. Schleiermacher views an individual expression as a "moment of life breaking forth," as an "act." The characterization of the act of understanding as construal [*Konstruktion*] is reminiscent of Ast's formula, "the re-creation of a creation" (§80, p. 187), but it may well also be understood in the pregnant sense the word has in German Idealism, for instance with Schelling.

The same contrast between traditional hermeneutics and the hermeneutics to be established is treated in paragraphs 15 and 16 of the compendium-like presentation of 1819:

The less rigorous practice of the art [at first the manuscript read "the artless practice," that is, of interpretation] is based on the assumption that understanding occurs as a matter of course: and expresses the goal negatively as "Misunderstanding is to be avoided." [...] The more rigorous practice is based on the assumption that misunderstanding occurs as a matter of course and that understanding must be willed and sought at every point.

(pp. 109–10)

The early aphorism left open how the object of understanding could be perceived as necessary and construed, and closed with the proposition that understanding according to this maxim is an "unending task" (p. 41). Schleiermacher's exposition of these two paragraphs, however, places his concept of understanding in the context of his theory of grammatical and psychological or technical interpretation. This actual methodology[9] represents the most interesting part of his hermeneutics, a part which, as Heinz Kimmerle has correctly observed, has been overlooked by existential-philosophical reception of Schleiermacher and still awaits exploration.[10]

Schleiermacher distinguishes two moments in the act of understanding:

to understand speech in the context of the language with its possibilities, and to understand it as a fact in the thinking of the speaker (p. 98). Each person is, on the one hand, a locus where a given language takes shape in a particular way, and his speech can be understood only in the context of the totality of the language. But then he is also a continuously developing spirit, and his

---

[9] See Chapter 10, pp. 121ff.
[10] Kimmerle, "Editor's Introduction," pp. 27–8.

speech is only one fact in this development in relation to many others (p. 98). Speech cannot be understood as a fact in a person's development unless it is also understood in relation to the language [...], nor can it be understood as a modification of the language unless it is also understood as a fact in the development of the person. (p. 99)

Understanding thus consists of two moments and exists, as Schleier-macher says, only "in the coinherence" (p. 98) of these two moments. Grammatical interpretation serves one of them, the consideration of speech in its relation to the totality of language; psychological interpretation, which Schleiermacher also terms technical interpretation, serves the other, the consideration of speech in its relation to the thought of its originator.

Simplifying matters, we could say that the reception of Schleier-macher's hermeneutics by existential philosophy, as inaugurated by Dilthey, skipped over grammatical interpretation and took up the other kind only as psychological interpretation, that is, as a kind of interpretation that has recourse to the author's individuality, but not as technical interpretation, which finds the individuality of the author concretized in the basic features of a work's composition. In his introduction to the new edition of *Hermeneutik*, Kimmerle writes that technical interpretation in the last texts of Schleiermacher, the lectures of 1832–33, is no longer viewed

in terms of language, as the understanding of a technical (individual) nuance of meaning, but instead in terms of the psychology of the speaker, as a "moment" in the formation of his thought and its linguistic expression.[11] This final form of Schleiermacher's hermeneutics became the basis for F. Lücke's edition and was thus decisive in his reception by Dilthey. The objectively convincing and positive ideas in Schleiermacher's early drafts were thus forgotten.[12]

The attributes "objectively convincing" and "positive" will prove to be neither, but we will see that many ideas of relevance to contemporary hermeneutics are contained in Schleiermacher's theory of grammatical and technical interpretation.

It was around 1900 that the other side of Schleiermacher was taken up, the side that emphasizes empathy, or identification, and that claims to be able to solve the problem of temporal distance by such means, by the means, that is, of historicism. In his first Academy address Schleiermacher says:

[11] Ibid., p. 39.   [12] Ibid., p. 40.

It is a completely different sort of certainty [...], a divinatory certainty, which arises when an interpreter delves as deeply as possible into a writer's state of mind. Thus it is often the case, as the Platonic rhapsodist admits, though quite naively, that he is able to offer an outstanding interpretation of Homer, but frequently cannot shed light on other writers, whether poets or prosaists. For, provided the knowledge is available to him, an interpreter can and should show himself to be equally competent in every area related to language and to the historical situation of a people and of an age. Yet, just as in life we are most successful in understanding our friends, so a skillful interpreter is most successful in correctly interpreting a writer's process of drafting and composing a work, the product of his personal distinctiveness in language and in all his relationships, when the writer is among those favorites to whom he has become most attuned. For works of other writers, however, an interpreter will content himself with knowing less about these things; he will not feel ashamed to seek help from colleagues who are closer to them.

(p. 185)

I hardly need to point out that these are extremely problematic statements. To be sure, we cannot simply dismiss the role of subjectivity, or even of affinity, in the process of understanding. But is it a psychological truth that we best understand the people and authors to whom we are closest, the "favorites" to whom we have become "most attuned"? Valéry was of a different opinion when he wrote in his notebook, under the heading "Lumières naturelles" ["Natural light"]:

Hatred inhabits the enemy, sounds his depths, dissects the most delicate roots of the designs he nurtures in his heart. We fathom him better than ourselves and better than he can himself. He forgets himself, we do not forget him.[13]

Be that as it may, Schleiermacher distinguishes, on the one hand, the understanding that is based on knowledge of language and history and is independent of the subjectivity of the interpreter, and on the other, the understanding that is based on empathy, or identification. It is completely understandable that existential philosophy and psychology at the turn of the century would have responded to Positivism's overemphasis on the objectively given by over-emphasizing the subjective element of empathy. This makes much of the scholarship of that period unreadable today. Nevertheless, in Schleiermacher's concepts both of grammatical and of technical interpretation (which is either part of psychological interpretation or identical with it – his terminology shifts back and forth) a basis is

---

[13] Paul Valéry, *Œuvres*, ed. J. Hytier (Paris, 1960), vol. 2, pp. 684f. Tr. M. W.

established for an understanding of what is individually specific, but also of what is historically specific, in the medium of language as well as in literary forms and genres. It is here that the ground is laid for a kind of stylistic criticism and formal analysis which allow us to recognize both the individuality and the historicity of phenomena. In this respect, as Kimmerle correctly notes, Schleiermacher not only anticipates but at the same time overcomes historicism and existential philosophy. This does not mean that he has nothing in common with historicism, as the following sentence from the earliest drafts demonstrates: "One must try to become the immediate reader of a text in order to understand its allusions, its atmosphere, and its special field of images" (p. 43).

Schleiermacher began his second Academy address by examining Ast's treatment of the hermeneutic circle:

The hermeneutic principle which Ast has proposed and in several respects developed quite extensively is that just as the whole is understood from the parts, so the parts can be understood only from the whole. This principle is of such consequence for hermeneutics and so incontestable that one cannot even begin to interpret without using it. Indeed, a great number of hermeneutic rules are to a greater or lesser extent based on it. (pp. 195–6)

Whereas Ast insisted that the circle should not be unbreakable and could declare it broken on the grounds of the postulate of Identity philosophy that part and whole are not in opposition but compose a unity, Schleiermacher recognizes in the circle the condition of understanding. Of course, aᵉ sentence from the early aphorisms like "One must already know a person in order to understand what he says, and yet one is supposed to get to know him by what he says" (p. 56) shows that Schleiermacher was still uncomfortable with the idea. But the compendium of 1819 already contains the recognition that understanding, far from being obliged to try to break the circle, finds in it the condition which makes understanding possible. In §20 we read:

The vocabulary and the history of a writer's era constitute the whole in terms of which his writings, as the part, must be understood, and vice versa. [...] Complete knowledge is everywhere implicated in this apparent circle, such that each particular can be understood only through the general of which it is a part, and vice versa. And all knowledge which is scientific must be constructed in this way.   (p. 113)

Here, in opposition to Ast, the position is adopted that is taken up in Heidegger's warning that the circle of understanding "is not to be reduced to the level of a vicious circle."[14] But just as Schleiermacher was not the first to acknowledge the circular nature of understanding, so the positing of this circle has not always meant the same thing historically. It would be instructive to trace the history of hermeneutics in terms of the changes the notion of the hermeneutic circle has undergone, for not only has the status of the circle changed (from vicious to legitimate), its content has changed as well. In his chapters on the "Questionableness of Romantic Hermeneutics" and the "Historicality of Understanding" Gadamer has analyzed the two decisive turning points, in Schleiermacher and in Heidegger.[15]

What Schleiermacher writes in his second Academy address about the problem of the hermeneutic circle is expressly directed against Ast's solution in terms of Identity philosophy. His polemic bears witness to a philological passion for making distinctions that is often ignored in favor of the theses on divination and empathy in the traditional image of Schleiermacher, largely shaped by Dilthey. Ast, Schleiermacher argues, wants to understand every work of antiquity through the spirit of antiquity.

This formula could be viewed as an abbreviation of the method we have presented. For this spirit would be that which all productions of the same type have in common, and it could be identified by abstracting from whatever is distinctive to each individual work. But Ast specifically objects to this procedure. He argues that this spirit need not be collected and constructed from various works, that instead it is already given in each individual work, since each work of antiquity is only an individualization of this spirit. I do not contest that it is present in each text, but I doubt that it is recognizable without considerably more effort. [...] And if I add to this the observation that the spirit of antiquity is to be found not only in productions of a certain kind, indeed, that in addition to dwelling in linguistic works, it is to be found in the visual arts and who knows where else, this formula seems to break out of the specific limits of hermeneutics entirely, for hermeneutics deals only with what is produced in language. Ast's formula will thus surely fail to accomplish its goal. If we reflect for only a moment on the procedure common some time ago that was based on just this formula – that of using the technical language of one sphere in an entirely different sphere – then no one will deny that, even if such formulae are not a mere game founded on a clever notion, they lead only to ruinous vagueness and obscurantism.

(pp. 208–9)

---

[14] Heidegger, *Being and Time*, p. 195.
[15] Gadamer, *Truth and Method*, pp. 171ff., 265ff. See also the first volume of Wach's *Das Verstehen*, in which the hermeneutics of Schleiermacher and of his predecessors Ast and Wolf are discussed in greater detail.

10

Schleiermacher, II

Schleiermacher's theory of the two kinds of interpretation, the grammatical and the technical or psychological, follows from his thesis that understanding is composed of two moments: the understanding of speech as taken from language and the understanding of speech as a fact in the thinking subject. Each person, says Schleiermacher, is

on the one hand a locus where a given language takes shape in a particular way, and his speech can be understood only in the context of the totality of the language. But then he is also a constantly developing spirit, and his speech is only one fact in this development in relation to many others.

(p. 98)

Understanding for Schleiermacher thus is not identical with recourse to authorial intention, as it was for Enlightenment hermeneutics. The speech (or writing) that is to be understood is not merely a sign or vehicle of an intended meaning. It does not disappear in the act of understanding in order to yield to what it signifies, the pure intention of the author. In opposition to both Enlightenment hermeneutics and the hermeneutics of the patristic-Scholastic tradition, it is speech or writing itself, the linguistic concretion, that is the object of interpretation and not the meaning, the *sensus* or the various *sensus*, of a passage. The boundary thus collapses that had separated hermeneutics from rhetoric and poetics in the earlier models; understanding the meaning meshes with interpretation in its current usage. "The finest fruit of all aesthetic criticism," Schleiermacher writes," is a heightened understanding of the inner operations of poets and other artists in language – along the entire course of composition, from the first draft to the final execution" (p. 191).[1]

---

[1] This is the sense of the phrase "one should understand an author better than he understood himself" – a hermeneutic topos on the history of which Bollnow has written a worthwhile study. See Otto Friedrich Bollnow, "Was heißt, einen Schriftsteller besser verstehen, als er sich selber verstanden hat?" in Bollnow, *Das*

The first principle of Schleiermacher's theory of interpretation is that an utterance is to be regarded from a dual perspective: it is something individual that can be understood only by knowing both its author as a whole and its language as a whole, only by placing it back in that double field of tension whose point of contact it is. Grammatical interpretation establishes its relation to language, technical-psychological interpretation its relation to thought. Now it is obvious that a dual notion such as this will only be convincing if the two types of interpretation are related to each other. After we have examined both types of interpretation in their main outlines we will try to determine the relationship Schleiermacher establishes between them.

A coherent presentation of his theory of grammatical interpretation may be found in the compendium of 1819. It begins with two rules of grammatical interpretation that have been basic to hermeneutics since its origin in antiquity:

First canon: Anything that requires closer determination in a given utterance must be determined on the basis of the linguistic field common to the author and his original public. (p. 117) Second canon: The meaning of each word in a given passage must be determined on the basis of its position [*Zusammensein*] with respect to the words that surround it.   (p. 127)

Both rules serve to delimit the context of the whole on the basis of which the meaning of an individual word is to be determined, just as the individual word in turn helps to determine this context. The first rule refers to the linguistic system, the historical stage of the language, or more precisely that slice of it that enables an author to communicate with the readers he is addressing. The second rule refers to the system that the sentence itself represents. In the terminology of modern linguistics, the first canon has to do with the dimension of *langue*, the second with that of *parole*. If we consider which words from the one dimension and which from the other can help to delimit the meaning of a word, there results a further distinction: from the linguistic system it is the words that can be substituted for the word to be defined – parallel passages – and from the system of the sentence it is those words with which the word in question has combined to form a sentence. We have here named the two relationships that Saussure was the first to give clear expression to and that are among the most

Verstehen. Drei Aufsätze zur Theorie der Geisteswissenschaften (Mainz, 1949), pp. 7–33.

important elements of our contemporary conception of language: the paradigmatic and syntagmatic relations. Schleiermacher speaks of two kinds of context: the "whole context," or linguistic system, and the "immediate context," or sentence (p. 54). The fundamental difference in the relationship of the individual word to these two systems that Saussure was the first to define clearly does not seem to have been thematized by Schleiermacher, although he takes the distinction into account in the early aphorisms of 1805 and 1809 when he writes: "There are two types of determination, the exclusive, from the whole context, and the thetic, from the immediate context" (p. 54). Exclusion is the method associated with the paradigmatic relation by which is determined, as it were, experimentally, which equivalent words can be substituted for the word to be defined and which cannot. The meaning of the word in question becomes more precise as one after another of the equivalent words, which form a paradigm, is excluded as meaning something else. In contrast, the syntagmatic relation, which the word to be defined has entered into with other words in the sentence, can facilitate a positive, or thetic definition. Although Schleiermacher did not distinguish as precisely as Saussure between these two kinds of relationship, the paradigmatic and the syntagmatic, this opposition did seem to him to be one of three fundamental oppositions, and he made these the chief principle of classification in his theory of grammatical interpretation. (The other two are the opposition between the formal and the material and that between qualitative and quantitative understanding.)[2]

First, however, we must mention some of the questions Schleiermacher addresses in his discussion of the two canons. We will pass over the numerous sections in which he applies the hermeneutic principles to the New Testament. This procedure is to some extent justified, for we are concerned with Schleiermacher's contribution to *general* hermeneutics and with the applicability of his theory to *literary* hermeneutics, but it is also problematic, for while his theory is intended to supersede specialized hermeneutics, it has its empirical foundation in exegesis of the New Testament. A more thorough study of his ideas could not ignore the theological excursuses.

One initial question has to do with how to identify a text's original readers, for the first canon states that a closer determination of its meaning "must be decided on the basis of the linguistic field common

[2] See below, pp. 127ff.

to the author and his original audience" (p. 117). What kind of readers an author had in mind can be determined, according to Schleiermacher, only from his writing. We can gain an initial delimitation of the field common to the author and his audience through a cursory reading; however, determination of the common field must "be continued throughout the process of interpretation, and it is completed only when the interpretation itself is concluded" (p. 118) – a clear manifestation of the hermeneutic circle. As apparent exceptions to the first canon, Schleiermacher mentions archaic and technical expressions.

Archaisms lie outside the immediate linguistic field of the author as well as his readers. They are used in order to make the past present – in writing more than in speaking, in poetry more than in prose. [...] *Technical expressions* occur even in the most popular genres, as for example in legal and didactic speeches, the latter even when not all listeners understand.   (p. 118)

From this it follows first that grammatical interpretation must always take into account the genre to which the discourse to be interpreted belongs – an important principle of literary hermeneutics especially, which was touched on in the context of the work of Chladenius. It follows, secondly, that we cannot automatically decide the meaning of a passage on the basis of the audience we have defined, since it is possible that an author "does not always have his entire audience in mind." Consequently, Schleiermacher adds, this rule too is one "whose successful application depends on the interpreter's sensitivity" (p. 118).

One further limitation should be added to those Schleiermacher places on the validity, or practicability, of the first canon. We must not only distinguish between the specific audiences; we must also bear in mind that the degree to which a text is specific to an audience is not constant, but varies according to genre and historical epoch. This becomes clear when we compare a poem from the eighteenth century with one from the twentieth, or a poem from the twentieth century with a play of the same period which is not only dependent in performance on reception by an audience, but also depends on the fiction that the dramatis personae speak with one another.

A second question to which Schleiermacher makes repeated reference in his various drafts, and always with strong emphasis, has to do with the ostensible distinction between literal and figurative meaning as it is used by dictionaries to classify the multiple meanings of a given word. In the compendium of 1819 we read:

This opposition [between literal and figurative meaning] disappears on closer scrutiny. In similes two parallel series of thoughts are connected. Each word stands in its own series and that alone should be taken into account. It thus retains its meaning. In metaphors this connection is only suggested, and often only a single aspect of the concept is foregrounded. For example, *coma arborum* is foliage, but *coma* still means hair. [...] Such a single usage of the word does not yield meaning, and usually the entire phrase must be given.

(pp. 119–20)

In the context of a theory of metaphor, which to my way of thinking belongs among the most important desiderata of general literary studies, this proposition would have to be discussed thoroughly. It is mentioned here primarily because it marks the boundary between grammatical and technical interpretation and thus can help to answer the question of how the two types of interpretation are related. In his first draft on hermeneutics, from the period between 1810 and 1819, Schleiermacher writes:

That one confuses what belongs to technical interpretation with what belongs to grammatical interpretation. Included here are most metaphors that serve as explanations [*Epexegese*], such as *coma arborum, tela solis,* where the transported words retain their literal meaning [hair, arrow] and exercise their effect only through a combination of ideas, on which the writer counts. Similarly with technical allusions: plays on words, the use of proverbs, of allegory, where grammatical interpretation is entirely appropriate and the question as to what the writer actually meant belongs to technical interpretation. The most common example here is when the thought itself, as it is rendered by grammatical interpretation, is not part of what is represented but only part of the representation, itself becomes a sign. Where and how this occurs can be discovered only by technical interpretation. (p. 74)

The relationship between grammatical and technical interpretation seems here to be one of a division of labor.

But these sentences are important for another reason besides what they have to say about metaphor. They suggest an answer to the difficult question of how the theory of different types of interpretation (in Schleiermacher they are grammatical and technical-psychological; in Ast and Wolf there appears a classification that differs in content but is formally similar; and the same may be said of Schleiermacher's most important successor, August Boeckh)[3] relates to the earlier patristic-Scholastic theory of manifold textual meaning. The fact that in the

---

[3] Philip August Boeckh, *Enzyklopädie und Methodologie der philologischen Wissenschaften,* ed. Ernst Bratuscheck, pt. 1: *Formale Theorie der philologischen Wissenschaft,* 2nd edn. (Leipzig, 1886; rpt. Darmstadt, 1966).

course of the history of hermeneutics the one notion replaces the other as a principle of classification does not mean that the more recent notion has any reference whatsoever to the earlier one. Still, we must inquire into the relationship on account of the fact that the concept of grammatical-historical interpretation already appears in the old hermeneutics and there has as its goal determination of the *sensus litteralis*, whereas allegorical interpretation inquires into the *sensus spiritualis*. It is hard to believe that the new hermeneutics created by Schleiermacher and his immediate predecessors took over the concept of grammatical-historical interpretation without making specific reference, however critical, to the old hermeneutics. If the sentences just cited shed light on this question, it is because they insist that even in the case of metaphor and allegory, the meaning that grammatical interpretation yields is literal and not figurative, whereas the figurative meaning can be determined only by technical interpretation because the figurative meaning owes its existence to combination (e.g., of *telum* [arrow] and *sol* [sun]) and not to a supposed doubling of the meaning of *telum* (1. arrow; 2. ray). This shows that the theory of the various types of interpretation does not merely replace the theory of manifold textual meaning, but instead negates it: the new theory is part of the anti-Scholastic tendency, beginning as early as the Reformation, which insists on the univocality of meaning.

This same intention is expressed in the postulate of the unity of the word. In the compendium of 1819 we read:

> The basic task even of dictionaries designed specifically for the interpreter is to identify the true *complete unity of a word*. Of course, the occurrence of a word in a given passage involves an infinite, indeterminate multiplicity. The only way to grasp the unity of a word within such a multiplicity of usages is to consider the multiplicity as a circumscribed grouping with a unity of its own. Such a unity in turn must break up into distinctions. But a word is never isolated, even when it occurs by itself, for its determination is not derived from itself, but from its context. We need only to bring the original unity of the word together with this context in order to discover the right meaning in each case. But to find the complete unity of a word would be to explain it, and that is as difficult as completely explaining objects. The elements of dead languages cannot be fully explained because we are not yet in a position to trace their whole development, and those of living languages cannot be explained because they are still developing. (p. 121)

If it previously seemed that Schleiermacher was a structuralist *avant la lettre*, here we are reminded of the philosophical premises of his conception of language: those of German Idealism. Nothing could be more at variance with the methodological principles of recent linguistics than positing the unity of a word which is not itself present but instead represents, as it were, the configuration of its various nuances and possibilities of meaning: an idea in Benjamin's sense of the word.[4] And the rationale of the absent unity conflicts no less with the working rules of structural linguistics. That living languages are still developing does not mean that investigation of them has to take their possibilities into account, to leave everything open. The object of linguistic study is not the future language potentially present in today's, but the current language system, a synchronic slice which admits no temporal dimension. If it is implied that this temporal dimension is future in the sentence just cited, it appears as past — again in opposition to the principles of modern linguistics — in the discussion of the original unity of the word. Of course the multiplicity of a word's meanings can often be explained by — is preserved in — its etymology, but what is decisive for a nonhistorical linguistics is precisely the fact that several *signifiés* correspond to a single *signifiant*, not the possibility of reversing this incongruity by means of historical investigation. Such a reduction would after all be purely theoretical, while the multiplicity of meaning continues to exist in the linguistic consciousness of the language's users.[5]

In addition to the opposition between "immediate context" and "parallels" (p. 128), which coincides with that between syntagm and paradigm, Schleiermacher recognizes two other oppositions which also function as principles of classification in his theory of grammatical interpretation: the oppositions formal/material and qualitative/quantitative. The first opposition, formal/material, may also be designated as a syntactic/semantic contrast. Grammatical interpretation investigates formal elements in order to identify the connections among the elements of a sentence. It investigates material elements in order to establish the meaning of individual elements. In his discussion

[4] See Benjamin, *The Origin of German Tragic Drama*, p. 34.
[5] Even the concept of the word that has an etymology and a history that can explain the multiplicity of meaning is problematic because such a concept of the word does not take into account the phenomenon of homonyms, for example, the coincidence of *signifiants* like "mine," the meanings of which — on the one hand the first person possessive pronoun, on the other an excavation for extracting minerals from the earth — cannot be traced back to an ideal unity. [Szondi uses the example of "waren" which, as the past tense of the verb "sein" [to be], can mean "were" or, as the plural of the noun "Ware" [ware], can mean "wares." — tr.]

Schleiermacher again and again encounters the interdependence of the two aspects. And his analysis of formal elements touches on questions that belong to the domain of the third oppositional pair, qualitative/ quantitative. The following example will give an idea of these connections.

Among formal elements Schleiermacher distinguishes those that connect sentences and those that connect parts of sentences. In the terminology of traditional grammar, this corresponds to the distinction between conjunctions and prepositions (although individual parts of a sentence can be connected not only by prepositions, but also, for example, by suffixes, say, the genitive suffix, "-s"). Among the elements that connect sentences he distinguishes between the organic and the mechanical, or, as he himself defines these, "inner fusion" and "external aggregation" (p. 129). "Although" and "while" would be examples of the organic conjunctions, "and" of the mechanical. But Schleiermacher now remarks – and *this* is what gives the question its hermeneutic relevance – that the opposition between inner fusion and external aggregation is not a strict one, that the one often seems to flow into the other. A causal conjunction sometimes serves only to aggregate, while the aggregating conjunction "and" can assume the function of organic connection, for instance, in order to express a logical conclusion. But that is only possible because in the one case the conjunction has "lost its true content" and in the other because it has been "enhanced," or made emphatic (p. 129). These are the possibilities of language that fall under the competence of quantitative understanding. Whereas qualitative understanding has as its object the distinction between word meanings or between word or sentence connectors, quantitative understanding is concerned with intensity. The two extremes here are "emphasis," a maximum of meaning, and "redundance," a minimum of meaning (p. 142).

If a conjunction like "and," which usually serves a merely mechanical, additive function, produces an organic connection, then it is a case of emphasis. If a causal conjunction functions only additively, it has become "empty," and we have a case of redundance. But since the shift in a conjunction's function from mechanical to organic is realized by emphatic use of the conjunction, the qualitative distinction becomes a quantitative one. Anyone who has ever tried to puzzle out whether the word "since" is being used in a temporal sense – that is, in Schleiermacher's terminology, mechanically – or a causal sense, that is organically, will not need to hear more about the hermeneutic relevance of these considerations. (The temporal "since" produces a merely mechanical connection because the temporal relation is external to the events themselves, whereas the causal "since" proclaims one event the cause of the other.)[a]

I will conclude these remarks on Schleiermacher's theory of grammatical interpretation by turning briefly to the broader context in which the concepts "emphasis" and "redundance" stand in his work. At the same time it will become apparent to what extent his hermeneutics is rooted in the exegetical problems posed by the New Testament. In the compendium of 1819 we read: "The maxim that one should take as much as possible tautologically is just as false as the maxim that as much as possible should be taken emphatically." Schleiermacher explains as follows:

> The former maxim [take as much as possible tautologically] is the more recent; it is believed to be justified in interpretation of the New Testament because of this text's predominant form of parallelism and its relative lack of logical rigor; but this is mistaken, and in accordance with the above-stated propositions, one must give up this position. It is believed justified especially by any slight appearance of synonymy. [...] The latter maxim [take as much as possible emphatically] is the older, and it is related to the view that the Holy Spirit is the author and that He would do nothing in vain; thus no redundance, no tautology, and thus the notion that anything similar should be taken emphatically. But then the notion developed that everything should be so regarded, for there is an element of "too much" in every word if it [i.e., all its possible meanings] is not completely exhausted in every usage. But since for the original hearers and readers the person of the writer never disappeared, and they could judge speech and writing only in accordance with the customary criteria, it is futile to resort to the excuse that the Holy Spirit had in mind all of inspiration-believing Christendom, which is allowed to judge Him only in accordance with said maxim. Since Christendom could have originated only as a result of a correct understanding imparted to the first Christians, this maxim is completely untenable.   (pp. 143–4)

These propositions contradict not only the traditional maxims of theological hermeneutics but also the maxims based on hermeneutic fairness in Meier's theory of interpretation. It would be interesting to take them as a point of departure for elucidating Schleiermacher's historical position, especially in light of the last-cited remark according to which Christendom – *qua* audience the criterion of interpretation –

---

[a] Szondi uses the example of the conjunction "weil" as it occurs in old texts. "Weil" currently means "because," with a very strong causal connotation; in earlier usage it could also mean "while."

is itself shaped by reception of the New Testament by the first Christians, who did not ignore the person of the apostles and regard the Holy Spirit instead as the author. For this represents an important step in connecting hermeneutics and the history of reception, which is one of the objectives of literary studies today. But we cannot do more than cite the following rule which Schleiermacher puts in the place of the dual maxim he rejects. This rule, which is of the greatest significance for literary hermeneutics, states that "the amount of redundance or emphasis that may be assumed depends not only on the genre of the discourse but also on the stage of development of the subject matter." And he comments:

If a subject in some area has already been adequately developed, then one can assume an average, and the genre of discourse will determine when and where one can expect more emphasis or redundance. But if the subject is still new and language for it has not yet been developed, it becomes somewhat uncertain whether the phraseology selected for treating it is effective; and where the language is to designate something specific, the author is inclined to ensure what is not certain enough by means of another expression. This is the source of the accumulations of words that are taken for tautology or emphasis. But the truth is that one should regard the expressions neither as identical nor as antithetical, but rather as units, and develop the idea from the totality of them. In the New Testament Paul shows this the least [this should probably read "the most"] because his terminology depends so heavily on oral tradition; John shows it the least. False emphasis has led people to join various expressions (renewal, illumination, rebirth) into a dogmatic system of c[oncepts], and that practice has resulted in a confusing, unscientific excess. False tautologies have led people to ascribe a minimum of content to expressions, and thus to give up the c[oncept].   (pp. 144f.)

What is important in Schleiermacher's thesis is again its connection with the perspective of genre and history. If we wish to establish literary hermeneutics as a material theory that incorporates the insights of historical consciousness and the closely related insights of post-Enlightenment poetics, then it cannot be a hermeneutics of rules that of necessity abstracts from the specific nature of the object of understanding, but instead will be a hermeneutics which expresses its materiality by clarifying the criteria that make a text in its specificity available to the understanding. Perhaps the most important of these criteria are historicity and genre in the broadest sense of the term.

I would now like to turn to technical, or psychological, interpretation and briefly examine the role these criteria play in this type of interpretation. It is all the more important to do so because the term "psychological interpretation" and the reception of Schleiermacher's work that was so profoundly influenced by this term and by the related concepts of "empathy" and "experience" give a completely false picture of Schleiermacher's intentions, at least in the earlier phases of his hermeneutic thinking. It is true that in technical-psychological interpretation attention is directed at man, at his individuality, just as in grammatical interpretation it is directed at language and its individual modifications. But even in the late Academy addresses Schleiermacher's characterization of the object of psychological interpretation as "the original psychic process of generating and combining ideas and images" (p. 148) implies the objective aspect of language as a medium of this generation and combination. This is even clearer in the earlier drafts and in the concept of technical interpretation and its central category, style, which of course relates directly to the use of language.

What is preserved in the transition from technical to psychological interpretation – a transition which, strictly speaking, represents only a change of emphasis, for the later Schleiermacher retains the concept of technical interpretation – is the notion that discourse is a fact in the thinking subject, related, not as in grammatical interpretation, to the totality of language, but to the totality of the individual and his life. The change of emphasis pertains to the investigation of this subjective individuality. In technical interpretation the accent is on the *techne*, on the individual style as a particular modification of language and as a particular mode of composition; in psychological interpretation it is on the individual's life as a whole. In the marginalia of 1832–33 Schleiermacher writes the following about what he calls the *relative* distinction between psychological and technical interpretation: "The former focuses more on how thoughts emerged from the totality of the individual's life. The latter more on how a set of thoughts arose from a particular thought or intention" (pp. 222f.). In the compendium of 1819 Schleiermacher characterizes the task of technical interpretation as the complete understanding of style. Here style includes more than the use of language: "Thought and language merge with each other, and a writer's distinctive way of comprehending a subject merges with his organization of it and thus also with his use of language" (pp. 148f.). As one can see, what more than 100 years later adherents of Russian Formalism, New Criticism, and the stylistic criticism of the Zurich school [of Emil Staiger – tr.] would present as new was anticipated in large part by Schleiermacher.

What elevates Schleiermacher above stylistic criticism as it was taught in the forties and fifties of this century is his eye for the historicity of phenomena, which modern stylistic criticism discovered only very late. In Schleiermacher the historical aspect does not appear *alongside* the psychological-technical aspect as something that should *also* receive attention. Rather, he recognizes that his goal of grasping the individual element of discourse, or of a literary work, presupposes historical interpretation, for two reasons. First, the meaning of the individual element does not remain constant throughout the history of literature. Here Schleiermacher confronts classical objectivity by drawing on the insights of the *Sturm und Drang* and early Romanticism. Second, the individual element of production cannot be determined unless one knows the historical state of the genre to which the work belongs.

Before technical interpretation can begin one must determine the way the author received his subject matter and the language [...]. The first task includes learning about the state of a given genre when the author began to write [...]. Consequently, exact understanding in this area requires knowing related literature current in that era as well as earlier models of style. In technical interpretation there is no substitute for such systematic research.

(p. 149)

The first Academy address distinguishes two periods, in a rather dangerously speculative way: one in which forms are gradually developed and one in which they predominate. The boldness of this construct is diminished by the addendum that the characteristics of the two periods subsequently reappear simultaneously (p. 188), which means that they are no longer periods at all. However, one insight remains decisive here, and that is that when a writer is working in an established form, we must know the form

in order to understand his activity completely. For even in the initial conception of a work the guiding force of the established form develops in him, [...] modifies [...] in detail not only the expression but also [...] the invention. Anyone in the business of interpretation, therefore, who does not see how the stream of thinking and composing at once crashes against and recoils from the walls of its bed and is diverted into a course other than it would have taken by itself cannot correctly understand the internal process of composition. Even less can he ascertain the author's true relation to the language and its forms.

(pp. 188f.)

If we recall that in the late eighteenth century poetic forms and genres as well as language itself were still regarded as a convenient vehicle of subject matter and authorial aims, we will appreciate how timely these insights are. They bring Schleiermacher's theory of technical interpretation close to modern poetics, as represented, for instance, by Valéry.

Schleiermacher did not always view the relationship between grammatical and technical interpretation in the same way over the course of the development of his hermeneutic thinking. In the first Academy address, following his discussion of the affinity between interpreter and author, we read:

> One is tempted to assert that the entire practice of interpretation should be divided in such a way that one class of interpreters, more interested in language and history than in people, would go through all the writers in a language more or less uniformly without regard for the fact that one will excel in this area, another in some other area. The second class would incline more toward observing people and would view language only as the medium through which they express themselves, history only as the modalities in which they live. An interpreter in this class would restrict himself to those writers who open themselves to him most readily. (p. 185)

This is a picture that still holds for literary studies in the 1960s. Although I am not of the opinion that a program like this ought to be dismissed out of hand as just a case of methodological tolerance, and I am too keenly aware of the dangers that a rigid disciplinary policy poses to human freedom and intellectual progress to join in the Dahlem chorus that is increasingly voicing this kind of objection,[b] I nevertheless consider such a liberal program theoretically inadequate. And indeed, as Schleiermacher originally conceived of it, the relationship between the two types of interpretation was not complementary — they did not share the work. Instead Schleiermacher advanced the bold thesis that

> the absolute solution to the problem is when each type of interpretation [i.e., the grammatical and the technical] is practiced in such a way that practice of the other produces no change in the results, when each practiced by itself completely replaces the other. (p. 100)

In inquiring into the rationale for this notion, one cannot ignore the polemical aims of Schleiermacher and the hermeneutics of his time with regard to the doctrine of manifold textual meaning. By basing

---

[b] Szondi is referring to the criticism of methodological pluralism which was being mounted by Marxist students and faculty at the Free University when he delivered these lectures in the winter semester, 1967–68. The Free University is located in the Dahlem section of Berlin. Cf. p. 93, n. 7 above.

hermeneutics on the concept of understanding rather than on the concept of textual meaning he creates the possibility of distinguishing modes of interpretation without presupposing a multiplicity in the material to be interpreted. Yet here again Schleiermacher does not stop at postulating an ideal relationship between the two kinds of interpretation, but instead recognizes that their appropriateness is determined by an historical index as well as by the genre of the work to be interpreted. He thus connects the classical and the most objective genre, the epic, with grammatical interpretation; but with psychological interpretation he connects the inventive, that is, the Romantic, and the most subjective genres, the epistle and the lyric.

Schleiermacher conceived of understanding as the reverse of speaking (p. 97) and accordingly defined hermeneutics as "grammar in reverse" and "composition in reverse" (p. 48, 56). If he was able to go beyond the limits of the linguistics and poetics of his time through bold anticipations of twentieth century insights, it was thanks, I believe, to this conception of hermeneutics as a reversal of grammar and poetics. For the reversal enables us to go back to the origins of the petrified system of rules of these two disciplines and their hypostatization of the data and to inquire into their premises and limitations as well as the interdependence of their facts, their dialectics. To this we are indebted for the overcoming of Positivism. Hermeneutics understood in this way is an instrument of criticism.

❖❖❖

Afterword by Jean Bollack

Peter Szondi's Literary Executor

❖❖❖

A future in the past: Peter Szondi's material hermeneutics

translated from the French by Karla Grierson

Peter Szondi's historical redefinition of the science of literature turns against the influence which the analysis of the Heideggerian structure of *Dasein* exerted in Germany within university circles, both during and after the Second World War. More specifically, Szondi's opposition is aimed at the model established by Heidegger's commentaries on the poems of Hölderlin.[1] The true stakes of the battle fought by Szondi for the development of a critical philology consist in the refusal of a theologically defined position and the principles it implies, which may be regarded as dominant, even in other countries than Germany, where one observes, in certain circles, a fascination with the possibility of surpassing academic and learned criticism.

Although the model furnished by the new approach to reading was borrowed from the philosophy of existence, it corresponded largely to the stylistic and methodical habits of traditional exegesis. It was Hans Georg Gadamer who was to include and legitimize them in his hermeneutic theory.[2] Philology as a discipline appeared to him as

---

[1] Works stemming from the reception of the philosophy of Heidegger by native German scholars during the first two postwar decades are presented and explained in relation to their origin in: L. L. Duroche, *Aspects of Criticism. Literary Study in Present-Day Germany* (La Haye – Paris: Mouton, 1967). The study leads to an analysis of the theoretical prerequisites in German and Swiss scholarship and contributes towards an understanding of the reaction which appeared in the sixties.

[2] *Wahrheit und Methode*, 1960; 2nd edn. (quoted here) (Tübingen: Mohr, 1965), p. 267 (now, see also *Gesammelte Werke* (Tübingen: Mohr, 1986), vol 1 and 2). Historical research concurs magically with the self-propagating display of tradition – with the "object," also called the "dogma," in texts and in language.

insufficiently representative of – and thus excluded from – the realm
of positive science, as well as from the "regeneration" of knowledge.
His aim was to separate the theory of historical understanding from
the so-called historico-critical method of the philological specialists.
The success of this new codification was linked to the practices in use
in critical literary discourse, but also to the positions defined within the
cultural and political sphere.

The part played by the "inexplicable" or by implicit structures,
lives on today in an almost identical form in other types of discourse,
which do not attribute the same permanence to the values of
"tradition" that Gadamer did, but which fulfill the same function of
erasing the set boundaries – as well as dulling the edge – of a
criticism, which would, as Szondi does, differentiate between its
objects.

The radical division established between "thought," as a noble
term, and that which was reduced, by the very process of the division,
to a positivist science of literature, is maintained, despite reservations
made against the violence done to texts, or concerning the obsessive
interrogation of a language thus ordered to hand over its contents.
This distinction continued to be accepted even when the anti-
Positivist reaction that Szondi had encountered in his youth, through
immanent or empathetic exegeses, had been abandoned in favour of
the auscultation of language, where the shifting of signs reveals, as in
existential philosophy, the intermittent structure of Being. The critical
analysis of poetic texts, which the prestige of religious reference
enhanced or ennobled, had the advantage of being strengthened by a
theory. At the same time, the ontological advancement, through a sort
of hyperbaton and overstatement, concealed a regression which
reduced interpretation, before it could reach the stage of analysis, to
a mere rhetoric of stylistic devices which was, so to speak,
transubstantiated.

Positive science being irremediably depreciated, reduced to the
common rank of historical fact, the essential task was to install an
alternative conservative legitimacy. Neither theorists nor interpreters
were willing to renounce the premises of the continuity and of the
unity of the Greek and modern cultures (German was meant). If there
was indeed a demand for a science of literature, the claims were made
largely in a spirit of contempt, the science itself, illusory and out of
reach, being jeopardized before being sought after, likened to a
collection of facts in order to be excluded from hermeneutics. The

science of literature was seen as contingent and banal. No analytical justification was required of that which remained, the auscultating, so to speak, of the text, which, by the grace of the hermeneutic circle, merely referred to the psychological expectations inherent in its own structure.[3]

Consequently Szondi's defence of philology is linked to an appeal for "hermeneutics" as a "science," based on a redefinition of its specificity (literary, historic or juridical) and determined by the nature of its object. Our present comprehension of the true implications of what may appear to be a restriction of the philological sphere is made easier by the fact that his critical enterprise, though he sets out to analyse *intra muros* the errors caused by the inappropriate application of the positive methods of the natural sciences to philological knowledge,[4] also examines, beyond its field, the persistent questioning of any and all critical processes applied to writing, as well as the postulate of total knowledge, all the more dangerous in its incorporation and authorization of ignorance. The textual interpretation was in fact reduced to a simple methodology, immanent in the literary discipline, by the claims laid to an immediate existential knowledge based on trans- and anhistorical categories; indeed they served to eliminate that part of textual analysis which did not meet philosophical expectations. The critical justification had fallen from grace. Hence the necessity, in the face of this discredit, for a twofold movement, allowing for a true advancement: the rejection of the refusal given to critical reexamination within scientific production, and the demystification of the external immediacy. Szondi's argumentation is fundamentally characterized by this double orientation, an effective critical catharsis and the battle waged against a form of ideological encroachment on literary texts. The boundaries of textual analysis were thus extended; the discussion of its rules was involved in this extension.

Although Szondi studied under Emil Staiger in Zurich, he did not adopt his conception of philology. The analysis of "style" in relation

---

[3] See above, Chapter 2, Szondi's criticism of those who claim to "question further [*hinterfragen*], as we say today, by evacuating specific problems in favour of an 'act' of understanding."

[4] See Szondi's essay, "Über philologische Erkenntnis," in *Schriften*, vol. 1, (Frankfurt Main: Suhrkamp, 1978), pp. 263–86, particulary the conclusion; English translation, "On Textual Understanding," in *On Textual Understanding and Other Essays* (Minneapolis: University of Minnesota Press, 1986), pp. 3–22.

to differences in genre, which for Staiger originate from ontological categories, and more generally, the ability to ally theoretical reflexion to interpretation in a relationship of mutual fortification, are the only areas in which Szondi retained what he had learned, and in which the critical positions concur: Szondi's viewpoint is in fact diametrically opposed to that of Staiger. For Szondi, emphasis, as a means to the deciphering of Being, very quickly became suspect, and he shunned it by confining himself to his over reading, particularly of Lukács. Szondi was thus indirectly exposed to the Heideggerian influence, which he immediately rejected, repelled by a pretension in scholarly works that both bore the outward marks of depth and aspired to be taken as literary matter.

According to the hermeneutics of the phenomenological schools, descended from Dilthey, the historical consciousness controlled by the subject is limited insofar as it is transcended by a call, which is less the product of a given work than of the dogmatic power of tradition. The interpreter is incapable of escaping from under its power without hindering the artistic or poetic experience; it is tradition which in principle prevails over objectivation in a "science of literature." With the advent of Romanticism, the defining lines of literary criticism were redrawn, and were to remain thus for some time to come. The interpreter remains subject to the call of tradition, his comprehension of the text is conditioned by his permeability with regard to the "voice," stemming not from the literary work, and even less from its author, but which makes itself heard nonetheless, somehow expressing the relationship between the writing itself and the act of listening as both an unity and a plurality. Thus textual empathy, considered as more than mere participation, which was obstinately rejected by Szondi, was theoretically justified: if a work creates by itself the elements of its comprehension, it is because these elements are inherent to a general, deep and common structure. "Grasp what grabs us"[5] was the watchword of this doctrine of interpretation, and so was the vicious circle not only accepted, but actually set up as an end in itself. The subject is bound by his understanding, "grabbed," just as for psychoanalysts language enslaves imagination. It is only through

[5] Adaptation by Gadamer (*Wörterbuch*, col. 10) of a quotation from E. Staiger's *Die Zeit als Einbildungskraft des Dichters*, 2nd edn. (Zurich, 1953; 1st edn. 1939), p. 11: "Precisely this: that which the immediate impression opens up to us is the object of literary research; that we grasp that which grabs us [*daß wir begreifen, was uns ergreift*], this is the veritable aim of the science of literature."

the refusal of predetermined knowledge that historical understanding and aesthetic analysis may emerge, for if knowledge is prestructured, and if its determination directs and controls the acts of writing and interpretation, the text itself can in no way delimit its own injunction. Considered as a product of the subconscious or as a vehicle of the sediment of preconceptions, the text would be of necessarily manifold origin, and the different points of view which it would engender in its readers could be consolidated only in the quest for an authority that would both possess and dispossess them.

If descriptive hermeneutics methodically depreciate the author's reflection upon his own creation, presenting this reflection as suspect by definition, it is because artistic production is considered to elude its producer, who is perpetually overtaken by the inherent dynamism, anonymous and collective, of a force which flows through him, and which he may not control without becoming a mere "artist," a master of artifice and of counterfeit authenticity. The more dominated was the author, the more unfettered will be the interpreter, who will discover, reinvent or simply invent the meaning of a work which was not subjected to an individual consciousness. As long as science clings to its methodicalness and to the will for objectivity, it is deemed to ignore the nature of its own knowledge, which would then transcend the analytical capacity of exegesis, as creation transcends the élan of the subject-creator.

The gap between the historical situations of the author and of the reader, instead of being first the subject of discussion and later included in the interpretative process, in other words instead of being first recognized, then appraised, is used against History. The rationalist discrepancy, belonging to the theorists of the Enlightenment, between the author or the text on the one hand and textual meaning on the other,[6] is exploited in favor of a trend towards absolute distortion, in that it testifies against History, in favor of a productive "historicity." Gadamer praises Chladenius for having not yet "suppressed understanding in the domain of History." If one accepts, with him, that "meaning is always determined also by the historical situation of the interpreter," the radical difference in viewpoint appears in his conclusion: " ... and, at the same time, by the totality of the objective course of History." The "course of History" holds the position which Szondi assigns to the interpreter. The same credo is applied to the

---

[6] Above, Chapter 3.

subject-creator and to the subject-interpreter, and is invested with the same dogmatic content: "The meaning of a text always overtakes its author." This discrepancy is taken to be the mark of veritable production ("authentic"), leading not to the author but to that which, in place of History, becomes and befalls, in other words the *Geschehen*.[7]

Thus, to cite a particularly enlightening example, the myths of antiquity are reduced to "mythical beliefs" and are mixed up with religious and even academic traditions, or at least the "belief" of the interpreters, believed to have always recognized this dependency. Phenomenology did nothing other than codify a practice used against the text. Tragedy, however, if defined as a "demonstration of myth," necessarily draws its meaning or its message from that which it demonstrates. Euripides strips myth of its truth, reducing it to the reality of contemporary events. Why the gods, if he does not believe in them? Theatrical effect of a man of the stage or demonstration of the absurd by a critical thinker? Art as profession and as disputation of accepted values. Whereas, in strict hermeneutical tradition, meaning is transmitted by legacy: it prompts and determines the spirit of invention: Euripides is then merely an inspired scriptwriter, a minstrel. But were the poet only a transmitter, he would not be worthy of his title. Similarly, the character of the Chorus in Aeschylus is considered to overstep his role in order to become the spokesman, not of the author, but of the myth, of "the divine causality behind the tragedy." In keeping with such a vision, all else is neither authentic, nor productive.

Jean Bollack, Paris

---

[7] *Wahrheit und Methode*, pp. 280f.

Index

Names

Adorno, Theodor, W., *Philosophy of Modern Music* 90
Akiba 7
Aristotle 10, 30
Ast, Friedrich 95, 109, 111–12, 113, 116, 119, 120 and n, 125
    Grundlinien der Hermeneutik und Kritik 96–108
    Grundriß der Philologie 102
    System der Kunstlehre 102
Augustine 71
    De doctrina christiana 69–71

Barthes, Roland 68, 115
Baumgarten, Alexander Gottlieb, *Aesthetica* 67
Benjamin, Walter 12, 127
    "Goethe's *Wahlverwandtschaften*" 79
    The Origin of German Tragic Drama 90
Bernheim, Ernst 14
Betti, Emilio 16, 34
    Teoria generale della interpretazione 1
Blass, Friedrich 5, 7
Blumenberg, Hans 64
Boeckh, August 125
Bollnow, Otto Friedrich 121n

Chladenius, Johann Martin 67–8, 74, 81, 83, 88–91, 99, 102, 111ff., 124
    Allgemeine Geschichtswissenschaft 14, 15, 20
    Einleitung zur richtigen Auslegung vernünfftiger Reden und Schrifften 14–66, 88
    Vernünftige Gedanken vom Wahrscheinlichen 26
Cicero 61
Crates of Pergamum 7

Derrida, Jacques 115
Dilthey, Wilhelm, 5, 8, 15, 94–5, 100–1, 103, 109–10, 115, 117, 120

"The Development of Hermeneutics" 1–4, 18, 94
Droysen, Johann Gustav 15

Ebeling, G. 2n, 10
Eisler, Rudolf 88
Ernesti, Johann August 112

Fichte, Johann Gottlieb 95
Flacius, *Clavis scripturae sacrae* 13
Fleming, Paul 62
Friedrich, Wolf-Hartmut 6–7

Gadamer, Hans-Georg 5, 12, 16, 48–9, 110, 120
    Truth and Method 1, 12, 34n
Geldsetzer, Lutz 46, 67
Genette, Gérard 115
Glockner, H. 88
Goethe, Johann Wolfgang 95–7
    Die Laune des Verliebten 23–4, 84–5
Gottsched, Johann Christoph, *Versuch einer Critischen Dichtkunst* 61–2

Hegel, Georg Wilhelm Friedrich 21, 68, 95, 99, 110
Heidegger, Martin, *Being and Time* 1, 4 and n, 88, 105, 119–20
Herder, Johann Gottfried 94–5, 97
Hesiod 6
Heyne, Ch. G. 95
Hölderlin, Friedrich 99, 103
Homer 5, 6, 115, 118
Horace 107
Horkheimer, Max 12

Jauß, Hans Robert 12

Kant, Immanuel 56, 74, 95
Kimmerle, Heinz 110, 116–17, 119

Lausberg, Heinrich 59n

141

Index

Subjects

Index

and the theory of signs, or semiology, *see* sign
traditional and theoretically grounded 4, 115f.
hermeneutic circle 1, 3–4, 39, 65, 100, 104–7, 111
breakable/unbreakable 105–6, 119–20
historical situatedness 20, 33, 49, 54, 56, 58
historicality 5–6, 53
historicity
of consciousness 5, 51, 130
of interpretation 48, 101
of meaning, *see* meaning, change of
of philological praxis, *see* philology
of understanding, *see* understanding
history
effective 12, 48, 57
philosophy of, and hermeneutics 101f., 104, 107
homonymy and synonymy 85–7, 127n

idealism and sensationalism 99f., 126
imitation
of antiquity 102
of nature 43ff. and n, 44n, 47, 58
interpretation
allegorical 6–8, 30, 32, 34, 49, 80
art of 4, 115
certainty of 25, 33, 40, 43, 56, 81, 83, 118
as the elimination of historical distance 5ff., 102ff., 111
and genre, *see* genre
grammatical 6ff., 22, 32, 49, 56–7, 116–18, 121–2, 124–31, 133
"psychological" or "technical" 116–18, 121–2, 125, 130–3
qualitative and quantitative 123, 127–8
as recapitulation of a text's genesis 106–7, 111, 134
recourse to the author in 28, 37f., 41ff., 47f., 56f., 80–2, 100, 111, 116, 121–2
and textual criticism 22ff.
see also understanding

knowledge, "vivid" 36–7, 74

langue and *parole* 86, 122
lyric poetry 43f., 47, 134
literary studies 3
logic 14, 29
literary 20

meaning
ambiguity 26

and authorial intention, *see* author
certainty of 33, 38, 40
change of 50–2, 82, 85
complete, *see* understanding, complete
literal and figurative 51, 58ff., 80, 83, 90–3, 124–5, 126
manifold or multiple 9, 29, 38, 43, 107, 112, 124–5, 126, 133
objective 28, 33
as *sensus litteralis* and *sensus spiritualis* 5ff., 10, 29–32, 34, 107, 126
straightforward and mediated 29–34, 36–8, 40, 43–6, 80, 91–2
univocality 26, 126
see also interpretation, understanding
"meaning-full" 18, 20, 26, 63
metaphor 38
and interpretation 64f.
theory of 20, 58–66, 125
method
analytic and synthetic 105, 111
empirical and rationalist 38
historical and systematic 13

Nibelungenlied 5

obscurity 23–5, 49, 54, 111, 115
types of 21–2, 27

paradigmatic and syntagmatic relations 123, 127
parallel passages 66, 86–90, 127
parallelism, word and object 87
philology 85
and aesthetics 4, 13
classical 102
historicity of philological praxis 10ff., 67
see also hermeneutics
poetics 29, 35, 44, 52, 121, 134
"point of view" 15, 20, 32, 48f., 53–8
psychology
rationalist 29, 40
of reception 29, 35, 37f., 40, 43

rationalism 26, 32
see also method, empirical and rationalist
reception, history of 4
redundancy and emphasis 128–30

semantic and syntactic elements 127
semantic change, *see* meaning, change of
sense, *see* meaning, understanding
sensus litteralis and *sensus spiritualis*, *see* meaning

143

Index

sing
  fruitfulness of 72, 78
  in the history of hermeneutics 68ff.
  and meaning 70–1
  natural and artificial, or arbitrary 70,
    72–5, 80, 91
  perfection of 72, 74, 77–8
  theory of, or semiology 68, 72
speech as hermeneutic object 113f.,
    117
spirit 3, 97ff., 111
  ahistoricity of 102
  Greek 97, 101, 104
  original unity of 99, 103, 111
  revelation of 98
subjectivity of understanding, *see*
    understanding

temporality 90
  and the structure of the work 90

understanding
  complete 21, 27–9, 31–2, 37, 40, 81
  as empathy or identification 117, 131
  historicity of 3, 5, 32, 33, 39, 102
    see also "point of view"
  and interpretation 100, 121
  objectivity of, *see* meaning, objective
  as re-creation of a creation, *see*
    interpretation as recapitulation of a
    text's genesis
  subjectivity of 32
  as an unfolding 106
  unity of the process of 38
  see also meaning